Waterford Whispers News

Gill Books

Gill Books
Hume Avenue
Park West
Dublin 12
www.gillbooks.ie

Gill Books is an imprint of M.H. Gill & Co.

978 07171 8555 9

Designed by seagulls.net
Printed by BZ Graf, Poland

Waterford Whispers News is a satirical newspaper and comedy website published by Waterford Whispers News. Waterford Whispers News uses invented names in all the stories in this book, except in cases when public figures are being satirised. Any other use of real names is accidental and coincidental.

For permission to reproduce photographs, the author and publisher gratefully acknowledge the following: © Alamy: 6, 9, 10, 11, 12, 18T, 20T, 23, 27L, 34, 48, 69, 72L, 82, 86R, 87, 89R, 91T, 92C, 93, 98R, 99, 100, 101T, 117, 139R, 140, 144T, 144B, 146; © Freepiks: 41, 46, 157; © Google Maps: 54; © INPHO/James Crombie: 145; © iStock/Getty Images Premium: 7, 8B, 10, 13T, 14, 15, 17, 18B, 20B, 25, 26, 27R, 28B, 29R, 30, 32, 33, 36, 37, 38, 39B, 40, 42B, 43, 45, 49R, 51, 52, 53, 55, 56, 60, 62, 63, 64, 65, 66, 67, 68, 71, 73BC, 74, 75, 76, 77, 79R, 80, 81, 83, 86L, 90, 92B, 95T, 96, 97L, 98L, 101B, 102, 104, 105, 106, 107, 110, 111, 112B, 113, 114, 115, 116T, 118, 119, 121, 122, 123, 124, 125B, 127, 129, 130, 131, 132B, 134, 136, 137, 138, 146, 147, 153, 154, 155, 159, 164, 165, 167, 169, 170; © Jane Barlow/PA Archive/PA Images: 19; © Pixabay: 142; © Shutterstock Premier: 4, 5, 8T, 13B, 16, 21, 22, 24, 28T, 39T, 42T, 44, 47, 49L, 50, 56, 57, 58, 59, 60, 70, 72R, 73BR, 79L, 84, 88, 91C, 94, 95B, 97R, 108, 109, 112T, 119, 120, 125T, 126, 128, 132T, 133, 139L, 141, 143, 144C, 148, 149, 150, 152, 161, 163, 168; © Rob Pinney/LNP/Shutterstock: 78L; WikiCommons: 29L, 78R, 89L, 166; WikiHow: 160.

The author and publisher have made every effort to trace all copyright holders, but if any have been inadvertently overlooked we would be pleased to make the necessary arrangement at the first opportunity.

The paper used in this book comes from the wood pulp of managed forests. For every tree felled, at least one tree is planted, thereby renewing natural resources.

ACKNOWLEDGEMENTS

I would like to thank my co-writers Karl Moylan and Gerry McBride for all their hard work, and Rory Thompson for his beautiful cover illustration. Thanks to Alan McCabe on drums. Ally Grace on bass. And a big massive huge thank you to our readers for sharing our content online and making us laugh uncontrollably at yer brilliant comments.

ABOUT THE AUTHOR

Colm Williamson created *Waterford Whispers News* in 2009 when he was unemployed. Though it began as a hobby, with Colm sharing stories with family and friends, his unique brand of topical, distinctly Irish satire quickly attracted thousands of fans. Now, *Waterford Whispers News* has over 635,000 Facebook, 200,000 Twitter, and 40,000 Instagram followers, and an average of 4 million page views on the website every month. Colm runs *Waterford Whispers News* from his home town of Tramore in Co. Waterford.

CONTENTS

LETTER FROM THE EDITOR

Dear Reader,

Declan O'Ryan here, owner of WWN, YesterdayFM, The Evening Echo Chamber and 400 other minor media companies you don't need to worry your little head about.

I've been asked to write to you regarding your continued support for Waterford Whispers News over the last 12 months, which I've reluctantly agreed to, despite you not paying a single penny in that time. But you bought this book, which I suppose is a start, so thanks for that.

With the half-arsed back-patting over, I would like you to join me in reflection on the eventful year gone by and indulge yourself in my superior vocabulary and stunning insight.

Like the previous years of its existence, the Irish government wasn't short of scandals in 2019 as it immediately leapt into the New Year with news of a giant €1.7 billion children's hospital bill for you taxpayers. Being a Maltese resident, I can't imagine how that feels, but I do believe I wouldn't be happy if I were a middle to low earner, slaving away, giving a quarter of my wages to incompetent millionaires to mismanage. It must be annoying, but I'm sure everyone is gearing up for a massive protest over it, once the global warming kicks in and the weather picks up.

Just when we thought it couldn't break any more unwanted targets, 2019 saw our health system hit the 10,000 patient trolley barrier in April, with the HSE reaching an incompetence level of Mach 10, followed shortly by a Mach 15 CervicalCheck crisis. Luckily the government was on hand to split it up into six, solving just about everything wrong with our never-ending scandal machine: the HSE.

Thankfully for us publishers, Brexit was the gift that kept on giving this year; we made an absolute fortune from Britain's demise and the new yacht is a sight to behold. No doubt Boris will give us endless meat to pick from and hopefully this profitable disaster will continue for another few years. I often ask myself how news and media would survive without keeping you all in a constant state of fear and chronic anxiety. The quick answer is it wouldn't, and all you people would be living together in blissful harmony. Yuk. Without Brexit, tensions in Iran, and continually splitting you all through cleverly divisive articles on gender and racial bias, we'd be up the utopia creek without a hovercraft.

Like the *Game of Thrones* finale, the left and right fought it out from the keyboard trenches, each as entertainingly irritating as the other. Strung out on the lack of divisive referenda this year, they took it to the beaches of the Google HQ battlefield, where we learned that hate speech is free speech, while the left is always right and the right had never left.

Never before have we been so connected yet so far apart and, to be honest, long may it last, because without you self-righteous idiots bickering in our comments sections we wouldn't appear in anyone's newsfeeds, so I'd like to personally thank you for that. Remember, you're a very small cog in a very large, complicated wheel that's careering down a hill destroying every organic thing in its path, and we couldn't do it without you.

Like other media outlets, our financial position is precarious and the margins are tight, but we would never let such a thing compromise our standards or interfere with our integrity, just like Heineken Zero with its clear, crisp taste. Drink responsibly.

Kind regards,
Declan O'Ryan

ww news

Waterford Whispers News

POLITICS

HEALTH

GOVERNMENT ANNOUNCES AN EXTRA ZERO EURO FOR MENTAL-HEALTH SERVICES

FOLLOWING on from the Irish public going to great lengths to raise awareness and fundraise through Darkness Into Light events around the country last weekend, the government has confirmed it is committed to adding zero euro to services, programmes, treatments, research, staffing and facilities that could aid people with mental-health issues.

'I'm not sure we need funding, maybe just more "awareness" awareness,' confirmed one government TD who made sure he was visible at his local Darkness Into Light walk, but nowhere to be seen during Dáil debates on the paltry investment in mental-health services in Ireland.

Ireland has made impressive strides in its attitudes to mental health in the past decade, which stands in stark contrast to the government, which today reaffirmed its commitment to praising everyone for raising awareness, while refusing to directly address ongoing issues brought to their attention by various experts, advocacy groups and charities.

'Was I actually part of the government that cut funding for mental-health services? Eh, well, whatever you do, don't look that up on the Internet to find out,' confirmed another TD.

'Of course, we could increase support for psychiatric nurses, help more people avail of affordable therapy, treatments and medication and so on, but we can't do that without first seeing if it will help us rise in the opinion polls. Anyway, fuck off annoying me. I'll see you at this yoke same time next year,' confirmed another government TD.

Health and fitness tip

While lifting weights, grunting like a pig being squeezed too hard increases muscle mass by 2 per cent.

WWN Was There

Waterford Whispers News

Easter Rising, 24 April 1916

What we said then: The disruption caused by these loutish thugs is unacceptable. Good, honest taxpayers trying to get to work and contribute to society, and these deluded scroungers want to destroy all that. The brave soldiers of the Crown must end this now. When apprehended, we're calling for execution. Please sign our petition attached.

What we say now: Did we get everything right? No, and we're happy to hold our hands up on this one. While we stand by the call for execution, our reporting may have overegged the amount of disruption it caused to tram users in Dublin. Mea culpa.

TECHNOLOGY

DENIS O'BRIEN'S INVOLVEMENT IN BROADBAND PLAN PROBABLY NOTHING TO WORRY ABOUT

THE general population of Ireland has been advised to simply carry on with its day and not worry about the government part-awarding €5 billion of your money for a national broadband contract to a company owned by Fine Gael friend and businessman Denis O'Brien.

Mr O'Brien, who was found by the Moriarty Tribunal to have illegally paid former Fine Gael Minister for Communications Michael Lowry £1 million to secure a mobile-phone contract over 20 years ago, miraculously acquired the substantial contract through his company, Actavo, and if all you eejits could move along there and ignore that fact, it would be great, thanks.

The Moriarty Tribunal lasted 20 years and cost the taxpayer over €100 million, but the idea that something like the National Broadband Plan resulting in something similar is, frankly, none of your business.

Senior civil servants in the Department of Public Expenditure and Reform strongly advised against the awarding of the contract to the one and only bidder but, again, you've better things to be caring about.

Despite originally acquiring the company under its previous name, Siteserv, the controversial sale of which is subject to an ongoing inquiry, O'Brien will now once again reap huge financial rewards, laying down the infrastructure needed to supply over half a million of you culchies with fibre-powered broadband, at between €5,000 and €20,000 a pop per home, or whatever price Actavo wants. But sure that's none of your business, either, so don't bother yourself with the facts, you big fools.

O'Brien – a serial litigator and central figure in another major investigation into the alleged privacy breach and illegal mining of data from the servers of INM, the country's largest media group – is now part of a consortium of business friends that will scoop the country's biggest-ever communications contract, a recurring trend under the Fine Gael government. But sure, that's Ireland all over, isn't it? And look, you'll do nothing about it, so piss off, mind your own business and leave the big boys to do their work. Good citizens.

EVERYTHING YOU NEED TO KNOW ABOUT ALEXANDRIA OCASIO-CORTEZ

OCASIO-CORTEZ is the recently elected American congresswoman the media can't help but talk about. A Democrat, but not kowtowing to the crusty centre-right bigwigs of her party, she's gaining new fans and detractors with each passing minute.

Here's everything you need to know about Alexandria Ocasio-Cortez.

- She is the youngest woman to serve in the US Congress and sleeps draped in a Soviet Russia flag.
- The 29-year-old is heir to the Irish watch-making brand O'Casio.
- Before becoming a congresswoman, she undermined the fabric of Western democracy by dancing.
- Ocasio-Cortez has called for a possible 70 per cent tax on income over $10 million, causing many middle-aged people earning under $100,000 to have fatal heart attacks upon learning of her proposals.
- Alexandria Ocasio-Cortez is an anagram of 'Kill Whitey, Send Everyone to a Gulag'.
- Ocasio-Cortez is fallible.
- Prolonged exposure to Ocasio-Cortez has been proven to make the women in your life hopeful and, in some very worrying instances, confident in their own opinions.
- Ocasio-Cortez is not well-versed in Middle Eastern politics.
- Despite claiming to advocate for the poor, Ocasio-Cortez hypocritically earns money.
- According to your irate uncle, Ocasio-Cortez is one of those 'namby-pamby leftie-weftie taxy-waxy gender-bendery feminist-wheminists'.

Suburban Dictionary

'Banjaxed': In good health.

HEALTH

CERVICALCHECK REPORT RECOMMENDS TREATING IRISH WOMEN LIKE HUMAN BEINGS

DR Scally's report into the CervicalCheck scandal has made 50 recommendations after publishing its 170-page report. Chief among them is the suggestion that Irish women should be treated like human beings.

'I checked up the definition of "human being" just to be sure. It turns out he's right – women are people, too'

'Sounds fair enough. I checked up the definition of "human being" just to be sure. It turns out he's right – women are people, too,' confirmed one person who was appalled at how some of the women affected were treated by male consultants.

Senior Department of Health and HSE figures will now act on the recommendations to 'treat women like human beings', some 956 other health scandals after they were first advised to do so.

'Y'know, maybe women aren't just a nuisance I have to bat away. Maybe their health matters above all else,' remarked one consultant who seemed finally to be getting it.

However, the idea of 'treating them with the same care, reverence and respect' that men receive would be a 'step too far', according to the HSE.

While smear tests remain vital and the best way for women to test for cervical cancer, the finalised report told of a 'total systems failure' in regard to responsibility over the scheme, as well as truly shocking instances of how consultants callously relayed the news to some of the 221 women who received an incorrect smear test result.

The report also recommended making the reporting of such instances mandatory, something Fine Gael, with the help of Fianna Fáil, vetoed in a health Bill put to the Dáil in 2017.

'Yeah, seriously, remember this fact when politicians come knocking at your door soon,' explained a spokesperson for voters' group They're Not Getting Away with This Shit Anymore.

'Lessons have been learned,' confirmed Minister for Health Simon Harris, reading from the same 'Apology Statement' all 25 previous health ministers in Ireland have read from.

A spokesperson for all those who should be held responsible has urged the public to refrain from going on marches or protests in support of the women affected, as then 'We would really be forced into doing something about all this.'

CLIMATE CHANGE

GOVERNMENT BURNS CLIMATE CHANGE REPORT ON TOP OF TYRE FIRE

RECENTLY the Climate Action Committee (CAC) report on addressing climate change made 40 recommendations on how Ireland should and could combat the damaging effects of global warming.

The cross-party committee has called for communities to be helped in achieving a low-carbon existence, to bring down agricultural emissions, increase renewables on the electricity grid, as well as a raft of other changes which would see enhanced power and resources given to the CAC.

Meeting around the back of Leinster House by an open tyre fire, the cabinet agreed to burn the recommendations on the fire, which sent spirals of black smoke into Dublin's sky.

'Are we all in agreement we need to ratify the decision to toss these

> **'So we're agreed, fuck this report on the fire and never speak of it again'**

proposals into the fire, seeing as they'll cost us votes? This sort of long-term focus, which benefits the people and not parties, has no place in Irish politics,' asked one minister, receiving a unaminous 'Yes' from his cabinet colleagues.

However, the government recommitted, in the strongest terms, to continue condescendingly praising young people for their protests and efforts to combat climate change.

'So we're agreed, fuck this report on the fire and never speak of it again, but redouble our empty gestures and say shit like "What an inspiration young people are" while actively doing the opposite of what is needed, wanted and recommended?' proposed another minister to loud cheers and applause.

Throwing more tyres on the fire, the cabinet stared directly into the black smoke and, despite coughing and wheezing, remained captivated.

Fullmindness

'Join the revolution today' Yoga can be good for the troubled mind. Sign up to a class and make sure to judge everyone there to make you feel a whole lot better.

FINE GAEL TDS START PUTTING ON INNER-CITY ACCENTS TO APPEAL TO THE POOR

IN a flagrant attempt to soften its image as a heartless party deaf to the concerns of the most vulnerable in Ireland, Fine Gael has begun to adopt 'rougher' inner-city accents in a bid to slowly win over the 'povos', WWN can reveal.

After consulting a variety of market-research companies in a bid to help boost its poll numbers, Fine Gael has resolved to mimic the accents of those they least want to encounter in their daily lives.

'The market research couldn't have been clearer. All focus groups, made up of many people from poorer areas around the country, stated their concerns,' confirmed one researcher employed by Fine Gael.

'They want a cut in the waiting lists at hospitals and other bullshit like that.'

Consulting with the wealth of research in their hands, the government resolved to meet its obligations to the public in full.

'Once we had put all that shite in the bin and burned it – the recycling bin, I must point out, we're not monsters – we all binge-watched *The Young Offenders* and *Love/Hate*, and started working on scumbag accents. We think the public will really respond to this messaging,' confirmed one Fine Gael TD, now wearing a retro 90s tracksuit while constantly spitting on the ground for no good reason.

Elsewhere, now that Louth TD Peter Fitzpatrick has left the party, Fine Gael will likely rely solely on convicted criminal Michael Lowry to provide the decisive vote in passing this year's budget. However, the party denies that the fresh delivery this morning of new roads and whatever else is needed to the Tipperary TD's constituency is anything but a coincidence.

HSE 10-YEAR CHALLENGE PICTURES EXACTLY THE SAME

IRELAND'S national health system, the HSE, stated it was 'absolutely flattered' after its 10-year challenge pictures were almost identical in 2009 and 2019, WWN can confirm.

The Health Service Executive posted two images late yesterday evening depicting crowded hallways with hospital trolleys littered everywhere, full of annoyed, sick patients waiting to be seen by struggling nurses and doctors.

'Oh my God, you haven't changed a bit,' one commentator noted, pointing to the underfunded, badly managed €14 billion mess that both Fianna Fáil and Fine Gael were responsible for allowing over the 10-year period.

'How can 10 years pass and nothing change despite the 10-year-old picture being taken during a global recession?' another person stated, referring to the continued lack of funding for psychiatric care. 'Even the fucking wages are the same!'

Welcoming the kind comments, Health Minister Simon Harris thanked the general public for their input.

'I just hope we'll still look exactly the same in another 10 years,' he jested, unaware of his blatant ignorance.

POLICING

GARDAÍ SECRETLY SQUEEZING THEIR NIPPLES UNDER STAB VEST, REPORT FINDS

A shocking new report into the peculiar habits of gardaí has found that as many as 93 per cent of members secretly squeeze their own nipples under their stab vests while on duty, WWN can confirm.

The practice, which was flagged in 2008 after the first batch of stab vests were issued to the force, has been hailed as a 'taboo' among members of An Garda Síochána.

'It first started during a routine traffic stop on the M50,' a brave garda told WWN, who wished to remain anonymous. 'The female driver was eating a snack box when I approached the vehicle, laced in vinegar now, lovely golden-fried chicken, too, and she was horsing into it like I wasn't there at all, so I kind of just stood there at her side window watching her eat – she seemed to like it.

'Naturally, my fingertips glided over my nipples underneath the vest, and that was it, I began squeezing them real hard while she tore that succulent chicken from the bone. The pain aroused me and I was hooked for life.'

The report also found that 3,879 gardaí were treated for either swollen or weeping nipples in 2017, with the large majority of them being male, aged between 25 and 45 years of age.

'It just makes me feel alive in this dark, deluded world we have to work in – an escape, if you will,' another unnamed garda explained. 'Yeah, the stab vests keep our hands warm, but they're also great at hiding our addiction. In fact, I'm squeezing mine right now. You wouldn't think it, would you? I hide my sex face very well.'

Following the report's findings, the government has proposed a full recall of all garda-issued stab vests from the force and suggested a new see-through vest be worn instead.

Bill's Campaign Diary

Veteran journalist Bill Badbody takes a leave of absence from his day-to-day reporting at WWN HQ to pursue a career in politics, in the hope of securing a place as MEP in the European elections. This is his story.

Week 1

Whatever it is, it's gone too far! There comes a time in a straight, white male's life when he has to stand up for what he believes in – an Irish Ireland for Ireland's Irish – and to, once and for all, quell the tide of scroungers coming over and milking the neo-liberal elite EU system for their own gain.

I will wake up the electorate. Some of them are so naïve and have no clue what is going on in front of their own eyes.

Met with my new campaign team today. Fiachra. Decent Irish family background. Had to give DNA as part of his job application – 100 per cent white European, so we'll get on just fine. Not 18 yet, so nice and cheap at €4 per hour. (Not paying the standard €6.86. Snowflake generation think they're owed a decent living wage.)

Will share news with Anne that I'm running when she gets home from her personal trainer session with that lad, Javier. Fair play to her, but how many times is that this week? And she hasn't lost any weight. Always in a good mood when she gets back, though, so that's something. Better than her nagging all the time.

Driving home after a liquid lunch and had to swerve into a ditch to avoid a farmer in a tractor. Road covered in filth, of course. Porsche's alloys absolutely caked in mud. Followed farmer to log his address. Sent him a €100 invoice for valet. That'll teach him. Surely these people shouldn't be allowed on the roads? A total ban on farm machinery?

THE HOMELESS

'I FEEL YOUR PAIN': BRAVE TAOISEACH LIVES AS HOMELESS PERSON FOR 60 SECONDS

A heartwarming gesture by the Taoiseach of the upper-middle class of Ireland, Leo Varadkar, has seen the humble, down-to-earth and genuine man of the people experience what it is like to be homeless for roughly 60 seconds, WWN can reveal.

The Taoiseach's act of solidarity with the 10,000 homeless people on the streets, as well as the other people the government removed from homeless stats in a bid to hide the fact the situation is getting worse, has received widespread praise.

'Wow,' confirmed one member of the public, whose tone suggested they didn't quite mean it in the 'Wow, he really gets it' way. However, many people from the Taoiseach's PR team have been paid to be moved to tears by his substantive stand with the homeless.

Placing himself in a seated position on the ground for 60 seconds with an empty mocha frappuccino cup in his hands, the Taoiseach went on to share his experience as a homeless person in a podcast with an online publication which targets the sort of people who fall for shit like this.

'I feel your pain, for I am one of you,' the Taoiseach said, addressing homeless people in an exclusive posting to Snapchat, Instagram, WhatsApp, Twitter, Facebook, Kik, Bebo and MySpace.

Just what the Taoiseach's decision to sit down for a minute means for Ireland's housing crisis and the homeless is unclear, but an aide close to the Fine Gael leader described the experience as a revelation.

'It's never been clearer to the Taoiseach that, having now been homeless himself for 60 seconds, he needs to commit to finding a way to shift the narrative, so it's made sound like it's really all just the homeless people's fault,' confirmed the aide.

Suburban Dictionary

'You wouldn't ride her into battle': Irish people have always been ahead of the game when it comes to animal welfare and we have an affinity for all God's creatures. This phrase was originally used when the Irish army discontinued the use of horses in official UN peacekeeping missions.

EXCLUSIVE

WORK BEGINS ON ADDING TRUMP TO MOUNT RUSHMORE

A team of 97 expert sculptors, with over 2,500 years of experience, have begun carving the fifth and arguably most controversial figure into the Black Hills mountains of South Dakota, WWN can exclusively reveal.

Many critics stated the government shutdown could halt the face of US President Donald Trump joining the faces of presidents Lincoln, Washington, Roosevelt and Jefferson on Mount Rushmore, but the president hired Mexican workers to circumvent the shutdown and begin the process of his face taking its place alongside the revered presidents of yore.

While Trump denies putting his own name forward some months ago for the honour of becoming the fifth

> **'The hair is the most difficult to replicate. It could take months to perfect'**

presidential face on the mountain's façade, which serves as a major tourist attraction, he has said he is humbled by the beginning of the carving.

Sculptors on the ground in South Dakota, including Manuel Domínguez, have spoken about the monumental task of updating the iconic monument.

'The hair is the most difficult to replicate. It could take months to

perfect,' explained the Mexican sculptor, hired on a temporary visa alongside 96 other Mexican sculptors who won the contract after White House officials sought to drive down the cost of the project.

'We think a total cost of $896 million is a fair price for honouring the president and all voters would agree. We made a slight saving on personnel by firing all the US workers, but this is America after all, so it's great to be able to achieve this,' confirmed White House spokesperson Sarah Sanders.

Sanders denied a shell company set up by Trump's children in a tax haven would receive a 'franchise fee' for the construction and maintenance of the face.

Community text alerts

The perfect O'Malleys with their downstairs curtains open and the lights on again. Whole street can see in. Showing off their new wallpaper. Border is awful. Yuck.

EXCLUSIVE

GOVERNMENT LETTING CALLS FROM RURAL IRELAND GO TO VOICEMAIL

DESPITE a variety of equally troubling and intriguing news stories involving rural Ireland and its recurring issues hitting the headlines these past few weeks, months and millennia, the government has maintained its tactic of letting all calls from the region go to straight to voicemail.

Regardless of whether the calls revolve around job losses, house repossessions, theft, drug addiction or woeful broadband, the minority Fianna Fáil-supported government has thought better of answering the pressing needs of rural Ireland, preferring instead to let the phones ring out.

'If you don't pick up the phone, it's like the extensive problems successive governments have ignored do not exist,' confirmed a spokesperson for the Department of Deaf Ears, whose main task consisted of manning a number of phones and ensuring

> **'If you don't pick up the phone, it's like the extensive problems successive governments have ignored do not exist'**

that no call is answered, under any circumstances.

'The government is not here to answer your call right now, but if you would like to leave a message, we'll be sure to ignore it until such time that your problem boils over and becomes a near-insurmountable runaway train of a disaster,' went the pre-recorded voicemail message in the vast offices of the Department of Deaf Ears, which has just one person working there part-time.

Rural issues have come into sharper focus in recent weeks despite the best efforts of the government to convince everyone that the nation's cities are the only places where people of any actual worth live.

'We announced some tax-relief yoke there two years ago. What they've to be complaining about is beyond me,' added the spokesperson, who was talking over the sound of someone leaving a voicemail about a spate of suicides.

Community text alerts

The Tramore Players' adaptation of *The Human Centipede* in the community centre tonight has been called off due to an outbreak of E. coli among the cast.

OVER 47 canvassers have been killed in the last two weeks following a spate of death matches between rival parties and independents, as the local and European elections loom ever closer.

Desperate to secure number-one votes for their preferred politicians, volunteer canvassing has now become the most dangerous job in the country, with gardaí calling on the public to report any death matches.

'So far, 12 women and 35 men have died in these one-on-one battles, with no end in sight to the madness,' Garda Tadhg Roche told WWN.

INCREASE IN RIVAL CANVASSERS FIGHTING TO THE DEATH

'Politicians should take responsibility for the deaths and should make sure that their canvassing teams do not cross paths, which leads to spontaneous street fights.'

It is understood that an unwritten rule stipulates that all canvassers, male and female, must fight to the bitter end to protect their turf once challenged while out looking for votes.

'The constituents cheering them on are also part of the problem here,' Garda Roche added. 'As adults, we should not be encouraging this kind of ludicrous behaviour on our streets. It's just not worth the loss of life, despite how annoying these people are.'

In one such fight today, a Fine Gael canvasser was battered to death by a Sinn Féin representative using a bundle of Pearse Doherty leaflets, putting Sinn Féin on top of the death-match leaderboard, with People Before Profit in second place, with 14 confirmed kills so far.

Fullmindness

Release your stress by undermining your loved ones at every available opportunity.

PROJECTED COST OF EVERYTHING SHOULD BE MULTIPLIED BY TEN, CONFIRMS GOVERNMENT

All but admitting that their current policy is just to pluck figures from their arses, the government today urged the public to stop taking their statistics at face value when they launch a public infrastructure project, promising now to simply state it will cost X amount and be delivered by Y date.

'Our advice is that when you see some glitzy over-the-top launch from us, and you hear one of our ministers proclaim a project will come in at a reasonable cost, just whip out a calculator and multiply whatever figure we mention by ten, maybe twenty to be safe,' confirmed a spokesperson.

The news comes after the Taoiseach told the Dáil today that the cost of

the expansion of the rural broadband network will be 'many multiples of what was anticipated originally', not long after the National Children's Hospital cost debacle, but before the inevitable explosion in cost of the MetroLink project.

'Don't worry, this sort of inability to be upfront and honest about even the most basic costings also extends into other areas of life, such as the 23 per cent VAT on vitamins,' added the spokesperson.

However, one area this strange inability to accurately state figures will not affect is the construction of social housing units.

'Oh, Jesus, no. You should divide whatever figures we trot out in

regards to that by 100,' concluded the spokesperson.

Elsewhere, Fianna Fáil confirmed they were so outraged and incensed by this latest, inexcusable malfeasance on the part of Fine Gael that they would continue to support the government.

THE HOMELESS

GOVERNMENT'S HOMELESS POLICY STILL HEAVILY RELIANT ON PUBLIC NOT CARING ABOUT THE HOMELESS

THE government's solution to solving the homelessness issue across Ireland lies in not solving, improving or abating it; rather, simply sitting back and hoping the public continues in its insistence to only care so much.

'You gimme a protest on a significant scale or even just one voter from my constituency saying "You've lost my vote" and I'll likely shit my pants,' confirmed one government TD who is not bothering with solutions to homelessness because at the end of the day no one is crying out for them.

'But right now,' continued the TD walking along one of the few streets in Dublin that is homeless-person-free, 'we think we can wait it out because no one seems like they really want it solved.'

While people who have their own personal stories of homelessness, or know someone close to them who does, continue to rail against a system that cares not one bit about them, the government remains confident in its assertion that no one is truly angry at them.

'And by "no one" we of course mean the types of people who vote for us. You ever hear of a middle- or upper-class person going homeless? No, of course you don't. Because everyone close to them abandons them and acts like they have leprosy. Then they're downgraded to a Sinn Féin voter, and no one listens to them,' confirmed the government TD.

Elsewhere, a large-scale, nationwide housing protest has been scheduled for a time that's just a little too inconvenient for you to make it.

Animal facts

The Irish for otters is 'madra uisce' but, on closer inspection, they look nothing like water dogs. An inquiry into how they came to be known as such was launched earlier this year and has so far cost the State €12 million.

HEALTH

GANG OF POLISH LADS BROUGHT IN TO FIX HSE

FED up with the state of the Health Service Executive, the government has turned to a crew of highly recommended Polish lads who claim the job is 'no problem', and should be finished up by the weekend, tops.

Minister for Health Simon Harris found the Polish lads through a neighbour of his who claimed there wasn't anything they couldn't fix, and that they were 'very tidy' and you 'wouldn't know they were in the place at all'.

Headed by the sole English-speaker of the group, a lad who goes by the name 'Piotr', the gang got to work straight away on all the outstanding issues with Ireland's creaking health service, impressing Minister Harris right off the bat.

'So we've got constant ongoing battles between the HSE and the Department of Health, real long-lasting grievances that go back for decades; the kind of shit that really leads to nothing getting done,' said Minister Harris to Piotr, walking him through a dense pile of legal documents.

'Okay, this no problem,' replied Piotr.

'And then we've got hospitals across the country that are dangerously understaffed and underfunded, leading to the longest A&E waiting times in years,' continued Harris.

'Okay, this no problem,' nodded Piotr.

'We've got thousands of women – we've fucked up their cervical cancer checks, and now we don't know where to start, let alone what to do,' admitted Harris.

'This, no problem,' an unfazed Piotr replied.

Community text alerts

Arthur Hanlon has just got the top score on Pac-Man in the local chippy. If you could all not try to beat this, as he has fuck-all else going for him. Cheers.

'We can't pay our nurses enough to convince them to stay in the country after they finish training.'

'It's okay. This we fix, no problem.'

'There's vulnerable kids we're supposed to be accountable for. We can't keep an eye on them at all.'

'No problem.'

'And speaking of kids, there's a children's hospital … I don't know if you heard about it.'

'We see it on the news. No problem. Many times we do this job, no problem,' said Piotr, turning to give a string of instructions in Polish to one of his workers, who was standing at the door smoking a white-tipped cigarette.

And with that, Piotr and his team set to work on the HSE, without even taking as much as a cup of tea.

ARLENE FOSTER'S GUIDE TO THE HISTORY OF THE IRISH BORDER

AFTER revealing in TV interviews that she is the foremost expert on the history of the Irish border, WWN sought out DUP leader and professional No-er Arlene Foster, as we strived to learn more about the frictionless, problem-free border between Ireland and Northern Ireland.

'There has never been a hard border, just look outside, silly,' Foster said from her kitchen in Enniskillen.

Seeking more incredibly informative revelations, we continued to listen to the fact-based lecture Foster was offering us.

'The Irish border was invented by the EU in 2016. That's a fact,' Foster explained while regaling WWN with a memory she had of 22,000 British soldiers patrolling a soft-as-butter border. 'It could have been a Philadelphia-like consistency. My memory isn't perfect.'

'The Irish border was invented by the EU in 2016. That's a fact'

Once we got Foster started on the subject of how there's never been any big issue surrounding the Irish border, the DUP leader continued to talk in the carefree, non-adversarial way she is famed for.

Consulting a map, Foster pointed to areas without Unionist MLAs and stated, 'I don't know what these places are, but their border is as soft as a freshly baked Christmas cake.'

WWN regrets that Foster's lecture was so brief, as it was clear there was much to learn from a woman so

committed to being upfront about the realities of how Brexit, hard or otherwise, would affect the people of Northern Ireland, the majority of whom voted to remain in the EU.

'Here's where the fadas are smuggled over the border from southern Ireland to be used on British letters and road signs. I'll admit, that is a disgrace,' Foster conceded, pointing to a random field she presumed to be owned by a Catholic family.

'We spent years trying to catch Catholicism in a net at the border and transport it back to the south, but it was useless,' Foster explained. 'Science has come a long way since then and we now know Catholicism is transported via tricolour flags, bags and T-shirts.'

Concluding her stirring insight into how everyone else is wrong about the Irish border and she is the only trustworthy voice, Foster said, 'There's something lovely and comforting about young British army men carrying guns and turfing people out of cars here in Northern Ireland, isn't there? A return to that lovely soft border would be nice.'

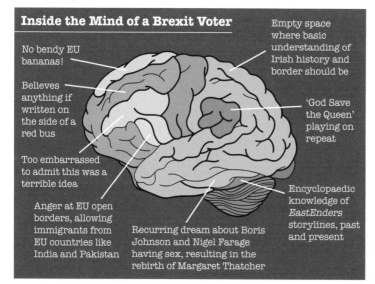

Inside the Mind of a Brexit Voter

No bendy EU bananas!

Believes anything if written on the side of a red bus

Too embarrassed to admit this was a terrible idea

Anger at EU open borders, allowing immigrants from EU countries like India and Pakistan

Recurring dream about Boris Johnson and Nigel Farage having sex, resulting in the rebirth of Margaret Thatcher

Empty space where basic understanding of Irish history and border should be

'God Save the Queen' playing on repeat

Encyclopaedic knowledge of EastEnders storylines, past and present

BRITISH PARLIAMENT SECTIONED UNDER THE MENTAL HEALTH ACT

UNLOADING 650 straitjackets out of the back of vans which had the name of a nearby mental institution written on them, medical professionals began the sad but necessary task of sectioning all serving MPs in the British parliament.

Acting in the best interests of a large group of people who have reportedly become completely untethered from reality, doctors confirmed yesterday that they had no choice but to act, after watching a live feed from parliament.

The disturbing footage, broadcast live and before the watershed, saw Theresa May lead the charge in voting in favour of rejecting a deal she herself had proposed and agreed with the EU. In the most disconcerting footage seen, May went on to claim she would successfully renegotiate with the EU,

> **'Imagine an unsupervised schizophrenic on speed and you're about halfway to what this lot have been acting like'**

who have stated countless times that they will not renegotiate.

'It's called a "collective mental state". Essentially, the entire parliament has caught a contagious case of dumbfounding irrational behaviour. Imagine an unsupervised schizophrenic on speed and you're about halfway to what this lot have been acting like,' confirmed one

doctor as he fitted a jacket to Boris Johnson, who was babbling mindlessly about a 'freedom clause'.

People detained under the Mental Health Act 1983 need urgent treatment for a mental-health disorder and are at risk of harm to themselves or others.

There were further unsettling scenes when PM May was carefully guided into the back of an ambulance in a straitjacket. Smiling to cameras and putting on her trademark brave face, May confidently and loudly proclaimed: 'Off to Brussels now to get that deal you all voted for when you voted to leave.' MPs, also being carted off, cheered loudly in support.

'Brexit will be a success. I have a Commons majority now. Nothing can stop us,' May added, before being sedated by a nurse.

Animal facts

An increasing number of red squirrels are dyeing their fur grey to fit in with changing squirrel beauty trends.

BLOODY SUNDAY DOWNGRADED TO 'DIGNIFIED AND APPROPRIATE SUNDAY'

THE Conservative Party has succeeded in its motion to rename the 1972 massacre in Derry formerly known as Bloody Sunday, following a party-wide agreement that Northern Secretary Karen Bradley's 'dignified and appropriate' remark in the Commons yesterday had a 'nice ring to it'.

Although the 12-year Saville Inquiry found that the murders on that fateful day were both 'unjustified' and 'unjustifiable', a recent report suggesting that four soldiers involved in the shooting of 28 unarmed civilians might face custodial sentences prompted Bradley to make her comments about the Troubles, or 'The Bloopers', as they are now to be called.

Tories across the party agreed that the vernacular used when referring to the entirety of 'The Bloopers' needs to be addressed, in a bid to help the healing process, now to be known as 'the forgetting process'.

> **Health and fitness tip**
>
> Staring at women wearing yoga pants in the gym does not count as cardio.

'Here's what we know to be true. There was a march in Londonderry to celebrate the free summer camps the British government set up for impoverished Catholics who didn't have the sense to live properly,' said Bradley, going through the history books with a bottle of Tipp-Ex.

'They met a bunch of jolly British chaps who were having an extended holiday in the area with 21,000 of their fellow dignified colleagues. There was a bit of argy-bargy, and then later in the day, 14 of the Catholics died from a delayed response to the Famine. I really can't see what the problem is.'

The move to rename Bloody Sunday comes as tensions continue to mount in the North ahead of a potential post-Brexit hard border. The Tory party is confident they'll be able to pin the blame for this on another group of oppressed civilains in no time.

GOVERNMENT PURCHASES 600 TONNES OF VIAGRA IN PREPARATION FOR HARD BORDER

THE Irish government has announced a €4 billion investment in the impotence drug Viagra in preparation for a hard border with Northern Ireland, which now seems more likely an outcome than ever, WWN can confirm.

Over 4,000 barrels of the drug were bought from Cork's very own Viagra production factory in Ringaskiddy, owned by leading pharmaceutical company Pfizer.

'This is a precautionary measure in the event of a no-deal Brexit, which will require the current soft border to be hardened,' Tánaiste Simon Coveney has insisted.

The shipment of the wonder medication, which is used to treat erectile dysfunction and pulmonary arterial hypertension, will be held in storage until Friday 29 March 2019.

'If there is to be a hard border, we are ready and waiting to distribute the drugs along the border, thus making it hard as nails,' the Tánaiste added.

Recently, the Irish government has come under fire for its approach to the hard-border issue, calling on Westminster to come up with its own plan for dividing Ireland from its land mass.

'I think this plan is probably the best either side has come up with,' concluded the EU's chief negotiator Michel Barnier.

EU LEADERS SWITCH OFF LIGHTS AND HIDE BEHIND COUCH AFTER MAY RINGS DOORBELL

'*MERDE*!' The words of French president Emmanuel Macron as he spied Theresa May walking up a Brussels driveway, shortly before pleading with other EU leaders to stop talking, turn off the lights and hide, in order to give the impression that none of them were home.

'Do you think she saw us?' Angela Merkel asked, now crouched behind a couch next to Dutch PM Mark Rutte.

It is believed that May had made yet another pointless visit to Brussels in the misguided hope she could renegotiate a deal that EU leaders have repeatedly said they will not renegotiate.

'Shit, shit, shit,' Taosieach Leo Varadkar said as May rang the doorbell for the second time in 30 seconds. 'You get used to it after a while, all the hiding. In Dublin we installed those lights you can turn off with the clap of a hand. Really convenient.'

Pushing open the letter box and peering into an empty hallway, May began shouting, her desperation clear in her voice.

'H-h-hello? Guys? Sorry, I would have gotten here sooner but my Flybmi flight was canceled because they've gone bust. Totally not because of Brexit or anything,' crowed the British PM, who could have sworn she heard some rustling inside the building.

'Just thought you guys might want to let me in so I can pretend I'm getting a good Brexit deal before I go back. Remember? Just like last week, when I did exactly the same thing,' May pleaded, now cupping her eyes over a window, staring intently inside.

'See, this is why we hide. Just listen to her. It's so pathetic, cringy and sad. It completely ruins my day,' Xavier Bettel, PM of Luxembourg, whispered quietly as he adjusted the curtains he had wrapped around himself as a disguise.

May, defeated, was ready to return to Britain with her tail between her legs for the 449th time in the last 18 months before she spotted something.

'Angela! I know you're in there. I'd recognise those sensible shoes anywhere. Let me in, guys,' May urged, as a panicked Merkel tucked her orthopedic shoes out of view.

Now in a strategic huddle, EU leaders and officials resolved to continue ignoring May's very loud sobbing until she eventually went away.

'FUCK THIS, I'M TAKING BACK CONTROL'

QUEEN Elizabeth II has called on the British army to storm 10 Downing Street this evening in a bid to relieve current prime minister Theresa May and her staff of their duties, WWN has learned.

In an unprecedented move, which will no doubt change the face of British politics for ever, the queen has insisted that she will now take care of Brexit negotiations with the European Union, the DUP and the Republic of Ireland.

'Fuck this, I'm taking back control of this bitch,' read an official statement issued to the media from Buckingham Palace.

'I'm sick of these incompetent, backstabbing politicians making an arse out of our good nation's reputation, sneering and jeering, laughing and taunting each other like a bunch of inbred baboons on meth.

'Britain needs a leader; not a yes-person who tries too hard to appease everyone except the British people,' the queen's written statement added. 'It's time to grow some fucking balls and take the UK by the reins again – just like the good old days.'

The vicious statement comes just moments after a press conference was called at 10 Downing Street by the prime minister, who seemingly forgot to resign during her speech.

MAGIC MUSHROOMS COULD SOLVE BREXIT, CLAIM DESPERATE UK SCIENTISTS

IN a last-ditch effort to avert one of Britain's biggest financial catastrophes, University of Oxford scientists have published a one-page report claiming that psilocybin mushrooms could help heal damaged brain cells in the brains of Brexiteers.

The report, which simply stated 'Magic mushrooms could solve Brexit,' was published at 10 a.m. today by a team of neuroscientists in what they say could be the country's last ever hope.

'No, really, it works on mice,' a desperate-looking Professor James Thameson told reporters outside the prestigious university. 'Psilocybin can actually change the way a Brexiteer's brain functions, both in the short- and long-term, and it can even cause the brain to grow new cells – Remain cells, we believe, we hope … '

The exciting new research pointed to the fact that psilocybin 'turned off' or decreased negative activity in the brain by allowing parts of the brain that don't normally communicate to interact with each other, usually, Professor Thameson stated, the 'common sense part'.

'Look, to be brutally honest, we really haven't done much testing on this, but we could at least give it a try,

please,' Professor Thameson pleaded, while handing out large quantities of mushrooms to reporters before being arrested by police.

'We're doomed. We're all fucking doomed,' the restrained professor concluded, before being thrown into a waiting police car.

Fullmindness

Find your inner child. Honestly, if you have small children inside you and you're not pregnant, you should probably seek out a doctor.

WE TEACH THIS PARROT TO MAKE MORE SENSE THAN BORIS JOHNSON

WHILE the media and card-carrying members of the 'I've More Money Than Sense' club paid to attend Dublin's Pendulum Summit and hear Boris Johnson speak in person at the Convention Centre, we at WWN instead burned our press credentials and chucked them in a nearby bin, before strolling over to the nearest pet shop in search of a more worthwhile use of our time.

As everyone laughed at funny man Boris Johnson, who recently failed to declare £52,000 in earnings to the British parliament, we walked to a branch of Pets 'R' Us.

Undoubtedly a lovable rogue, Johnson – a man who cheated on his wife, fathered a child with his mistress and then sought to hide the existence of that child through court injunctions – was terribly entertaining and funny in front of an enraptured audience. WWN was not there, however, as we were repeating key terms of the Good Friday Agreement to our parrot, who we named Smarter Than Boris.

Smarter Than Boris did not have floppy hair and did not make random, nonsensical references to Greek mythology, but he did now know more than Boris Johnson about Northern Ireland.

> **'People pay money to see this xenophobic charlatan?! Why does he ignore the facts? Why do they keep listening to him? Why is he on fucking RTÉ getting a free pass while spouting shite?'**

'The EU are firm on the withdrawal agreement. The backstop will not be altered,' squawked Smarter Than Boris, as he got to grips with the most basic of facts which have, thus far, eluded Johnson.

Being terribly, terribly entertaining and self-deprecating, Johnson, who during his time as editor of *The Spectator* commissioned pieces which claimed black people had lower IQs than white people, regaled the Irish audience with some witty anecdotes. WWN confesses we missed this, due to our decision to make a parrot more knowledgeable than a man regarded by many as Britain's worst-ever foreign secretary.

Smarter Than Boris, an Amazon parrot, continued to improve his vocabulary as we schooled him on the meaninglessness of the phrase 'Brexit means Brexit'. He soon displayed the sort of mental alacrity that has evaded Johnson, stating 'These liars can't deliver what they promise. Real people are going to suffer' over and over again.

We were only one hour into our tutelage of the parrot, but the results were encouraging. Less encouraging was the scene unfolding at the Convention Centre, where Johnson, who as Mayor of London spent £37 million of taxpayers' money on a garden bridge that was never built, was play-fighting with broadcaster Brian Dobson.

'How can you claim you'll give £350 million to the NHS? On what authority can he say that? He wasn't even a government minister at the time. Can he be sued for fraud?' squawked Smarter Than Boris, becoming increasingly frustrated by his intellectual inferior's behaviour.

We at WWN, however, soon realised the error of our ways. By teaching the parrot of Johnson's life – of failing upwards and repeatedly lying in a mendacious fashion – we began to send Smarter Than Boris on a path to certain insanity.

'He makes no sense,' bawked the parrot, slowly going insane.

'People pay money to see this xenophobic charlatan?! Why does he ignore the facts? Why do they keep listening to him? Why is he on fucking RTÉ getting a free pass while spouting shite?' Smarter Than Boris asked before he threw himself off a window ledge, refusing to fly so he plummeted to his demise. We quickly sought out our receipt from Pets 'R' Us to read their return policies.

Elsewhere, Johnson finished up his Pendulum talk to warm applause from his Irish audience.

Suburban Dictionary

'Acting the maggot':
Someone who regularly wriggles around on the ground, waiting to be eaten by a bird.

IS IT TIME TO LIBERATE THE UK USING MILITARY FORCE?

WITH tensions mounting between the elders of the UK's two warring tribes, as they slowly dismantle the nation from the inside out, is it time for the First World to step in and rescue the incompetent natives from themselves, before it's too late?

For too long now, this great country of ours has been observing from a distance the UK's warring factions and ignoring their idiotic savagery, even at its most disturbing levels. Once a strong and stable nation, proud of its unsophisticated political, social and economic prowess, the UK now lies broken and exhausted, like a lame

horse in a knacker's yard facing its proverbial final hurdle with a bullet to the head, while the West stands by nervously, its hands tied due to international red tape.

As with Venezuela, Syria, Libya, Afghanistan, Iraq and all the errant nations that crumbled before her, this sovereign union seems more divided than ever, while its people suffer the consequences of its own rotten regime, hell-bent on self-destruction.

Studying their language and social skills more closely, their buffoonery and mental deficiencies become far more obvious to the Western observer. Their vocabulary limited to a smattering of inarticulate phrases such as 'no deal is the best deal', 'take back control', 'the WTO loves us' and 'fuck Northern Ireland', such warlike phrases reflect their hard-wired prehistoric ideology, completely void of self-comprehension.

Mentally unable to discern even the most basic of facts, many worship an

ungroomed, blonde-haired tribe leader, resembling what one can only describe as a cross between a Neanderthal and a sheepdog, without, however, the organisational skills. What primitive minds they must have. It is incumbent on us in the civilised world to intervene, but to what degree?

Great moral questions might have to wait for another day, but it is clear the UK would benefit from Western influence, the kind that would put manners on this banana republic. Not to mention the fact that science has observed that their skulls are marginally smaller than ours and thus far less capable of processing information and applying logic.

As we have learned from our previous noble liberation efforts and battles, military force and invasion seems now the only option for an undeveloped place like the UK. Democracy must be delivered, if not for the sake of the UK, then for the sake of the Third World itself.

Suburban Dictionary

'Whistle-sucker': The opposite of a whistle-blower, a whistle-sucker specialises not only in covering up corporate wrongdoings, but actively participates in them.

REES-MOGG STRAPS STEAM-POWERED EXPLOSIVE TO CHEST AND DEMANDS WORST BREXIT POSSIBLE

STUDIOUSLY fanning steam up a copper tube via a Victorian-era foot pump, Jacob Rees-Mogg has finally snapped, insisting that it isn't enough to simply vote down a deal when there is room to also plan the very worst possible Brexit that could cause the greatest hardship for working-class and vulnerable Britons.

'My dear fellows, what hath transpired here is a dereliction of conveying meaning,' Rees-Mogg stated as he loaded gunpowder into a series of inkwells strapped to his chest, which appeared to be part of an improvised explosive device.

If his demands aren't met, the 18th-century Child Catcher will be left with no other option but to light a 12-foot-long fuse, setting off large explosives, which were ferried into Parliament Square via a steam-powered carriage.

Unsheathing a Gothic hilted British infantry sword from 1822, Rees-Mogg, speaking now exclusively in Latin, demanded that the people die of cholera, and have only a most rudimentary toilet and sewerage system.

The elongated HB pencil, who successfully grew back his virginity, says he will detonate his device if his demands are not met. Rees-Mogg became startled and angered by members of the media who gathered to take his picture.

'Cease your infernal flashing! You will not steal my soul with that devilish contraption. Take your witchcraft elsewhere!' he shouted.

Outlining his demands in full, Rees-Mogg, London's only adult chimney sweep, concluded by stating, 'Look, old chap, it's frightfully simple. The people want British soldiers killing their own citizens in Irlande du Nord and ransacking Rhodesia for minerals. Resign the Treaty of Balta Liman and put children back down the mines – just like the good old days.'

Bill's Campaign Diary

Veteran journalist Bill Badbody takes a leave of absence from his day-to-day reporting at WWN HQ to pursue a career in politics, in the hope of securing a place as MEP in the European elections. This is his story.

Week 2

Fiachra finally set up the social media page after hate-speech issues with Facebook community standards. Apparently a Direct Provision centre cover photo with a burning cross in front of it 'incites hatred' now? Banned for four days! PC nonsense again.

Found a lovely pair of leather Gucci men's shoes in the bedroom after coming home for lunch. Obviously Anne bought them for my birthday next month and forgot to put them away. Way too big, though. Size 13? Hope she kept the receipt. Said nothing. It's great to have such a supportive woman by my side.

Tweeted an Independent.ie article from 2011 about a foreign taxi driver assaulting a young Dublin woman. Seems to be getting traction. Getting the hang of this social media malarkey. Amazing the amount of like-minded people there are in Ireland. So many pro Pro-Irish pages to follow – a treasure trove.

Farage announced he's starting up a new Brexit party in the UK. Must do the same. It's time Ireland left the blasted EU. Time to piggyback on this Irexit shite.

Outlined my Indirect Provision centre plans, sending migrants off-grid to remote islands in the west of Ireland, out of harm's way. Direct is too close. Indirect is the way forward. My supporters loved the idea of using drones to airdrop seeds and water to them instead of wasting money on staff and expensive things like food. Let them fend for themselves in the harsh climate. See who's genuine and who's spoofing, just to get at our women.

Finished the week announcing I will not be paying any more VAT until the government stops mishandling taxpayers' money. This should keep Revenue off my back for the time being.

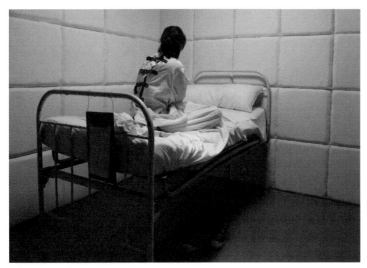

MEET THE PEOPLE WHO WENT INSANE TRYING TO FOLLOW BREXIT

THANKS to our guide on the ground, we were able to interview a small sample of the swathes of people who, gripped by an ever-maddening insanity, have gone mad trying to follow the latest incomprehensible Brexistential crisis.

In our efforts to reach these people, our guide told us of the world's largest open-air treatment centre for those struggling with their sanity due to Brexit.

'Britain', as he referred to it, allows people the freedom to roam around and interact with others. We were warned, however, to approach these patients with caution, as some had completely lost their grip on reality after valiantly trying to keep track of the latest ways their politicians were wilfully fucking their country into oblivion.

Curtis

'It was the government tabling amendments against their own amendments they didn't want backing on, but then they did. That's what did me in,' confirmed a man named Curtis, a former school headmaster. Nurses say he is no longer allowed access to Sky News, BBC, broadsheet or tabloid newspapers, as well as the Internet.

'I'm free now, though. I'm finally free,' Curtis said, smiling intensely as he went back to scrawling 'We did it to ourselves, you know' over and over on a nearby white wall.

Geoff

'What is the will of the people, if the people have lost all will to live?' Geoff asked us. Geoff, we're told, has been draped in nothing but a Union Jack flag for the last three years,

and mistakenly believes he has the solution to the backstop. 'We try not to challenge him. It upsets him,' an orderly explained. 'But how can you take a man seriously when he says the same things as Jacob Rees-Mogg?'

Romesh

'Shush, you can't see me. I don't exist,' Romesh told us as he stood in a corner. Nurses later explained that Romesh thinks he's one of the various non-existent trade deals the British government has alleged it will sign post-Brexit. That, or he could be the imaginary boats which Chris Grayling ordered.

Boris

'He's not actually a patient,' insisted a doctor. 'He just comes here and steals all the patients' ideas to bring back to the media and parliament.'

Casey

'At least I'll be old enough to vote on it when they give us the People's Vote,' a clearly delusional 18-year-old student shared.

Khadija

'Mention tabling a fucking meaningful vote again. Go on, I dare you,' Khadija said to us as she held a replica big red bus toy, which she had carved to make an improvised knife. Up until last week, Khadija was a successful CEO of a large multinational trading firm.

Theresa

'I'm glad it's all been cleared up. I feel the better for it. Easy to follow. We're headed in the right direction,' Theresa said as she walked in circles, perhaps the most horrifying example of Brexit-induced psychosis we have ever seen.

TV guide

The Nation's Favourite Piece of Cutlery: Following on from *Ireland's Favourite Folk Song*, RTÉ has run out of favourite things for the nation to show favouritism towards, leaving audiences agonising between the knife, fork and spoon.

Sunday, 8 p.m., RTÉ One.

'WE HAVE STANDARDS HERE,' SATAN DISTANCES HIMSELF FROM BREXITEERS

THE instigators of Brexit are not welcome in hell due to moral standards laid out by its ruler in a rare but concise statement from the Dark Lord of the Underworld.

Satan, known also as the Devil, confirmed that there was 'absolutely no chance' politicians like Jacob Rees-Mogg, Nigel Farage, Boris Johnson, David Davis, Theresa May, or any of those responsible for Brexit will ever set hoof in his fiery kingdom, pointing instead to their total annihilation following death.

'We've some awful pricks down here, let me tell you. But I would rather genuflect to God himself before I let any of those steaming piles of cancer-pus pass through my gates,' a worried-looking Satan explained.

'Even Hell has standards, and I will be fucked if I put my reputation on the line by letting those complete fucking arseholes start shitting down here,' he added.

Satan's warning to hardline Brexiteers comes after comments made yesterday by European Council President Donald Tusk, during which Tusk told the world's press there was a 'special place in Hell' for those who promoted Brexit without a plan on how to implement it safely.

'I'm going to have a word with Donald later this evening during his daily worship to me,' Satan said. 'Don't get me wrong. He's a good kid, but he needs to wind it back a bit and let me do the talking.'

WWN Was There

Waterford Whispers News

First sitting of the Dáil, 21 January 1919

What we said then: A woman politician? Ireland has taken leave of its senses. The female brain, small and crude in its dimensions, simply can't comprehend the male pursuits of politics, society and important decisions. By all means, allow their husbands to read to them from the paper about politics, but their delicate and fragile spirits cannot cope with such complex realities and happenings.

What we say now: It was, admittedly, a very different time then.

EXCLUSIVE

CAREFULLY crafting a post on his personal Facebook page, Tipperary TD Marty McDonoghue announced the latest local investment news to his tens of dedicated followers in the hope they will somehow believe he was responsible for it, WWN can confirm.

Despite having no previous knowledge of the €10 million funding awarded to local IT business TechTron, McDonoghue wasted no time in chiming in on the development, posting several pictures of the company HQ which he sourced from Google Images.

LOCAL TD 'DELIGHTED' TO TAKE CREDIT FOR FUNDING HE HAD NO INVOLVEMENT IN

'I am delighted to welcome the €10 million funding for local SME TechTron. Well done to Mark and his team for all their hard work over the years. It has finally paid off,' McDonoghue wrote, after googling the CEO's name.

'This is yet another massive boost for Tipperary jobs and enterprise that I've announced in the last few weeks and I am looking forward to seeing the completed project and the improvements to TechTron over the next few years,' he then added.

Like clockwork, dozens of people commented under his announcement, thanking McDonoghue for all his hard work in bringing them the good news.

'Fantastic news, Marty,' one constituent said.

'Well done, Marty. Delighted for TechTron and well deserved. Keep

> **'This is yet another massive boost for Tipperary jobs and enterprise that I've announced in the last few weeks'**

up the good work,' said another.

Happy with his progress, McDonoghue went on to check the local obituary news to see what funerals he could claim expenses for that day.

COMMUNICATIONS

GOVERNMENT RINGS 1850 NATIONAL BROADBAND PLAN NUMBER FOR ANSWERS

MINISTER for Communications Richard Bruton has asked the company set to receive the contract for the National Broadband Plan, Granahan McCourt, to elaborate on their plans to connect over a half a million Irish homes with fibre-powered broadband. WWN has the full transcript of the call below.

NBP line: Hello, and welcome to Granahan McCourt's National Broadband Plan hotline. Please press one for residential, two for business, or three for government enquiries.

PRESSES ONE

Richard Bruton: Ah balls, I meant to press three.
NBP: Thank you for you call. All our representatives are busy right now due to cost queries. If your call is querying the cost of the National Broadband Plan, we can confirm the cost as being €2 billion. For all other queries, please stay on the line.

PRESSES TWO

RB: Aw for Christ's sake. Three! I meant to press fucking three. Stupid phone.
NBP: Thank you for you call. All our representatives are busy right now due to cost queries. If your call is querying the cost of the National Broadband Plan, we can confirm the cost as being €2 billion. For all other queries, please stay on the line.

PRESSES THREE

RB: Finally …
NBP: Hello?
RB: Oh! That was quick. Erm, it's Richard Bruton here, Minister for Communications.

NBP Line: Ah, yes, Richard … Sorry I didn't answer your messages earlier. I looked at them and forgot to reply. Flat out here, you know yourself.
RB: David?
NBP: Hey, what's the craic?
RB: Mr McCourt, the people are asking me about the cost and what you're contributing.
NBP: Sure, you know the fucking cost, Dick. It's five billion-ish.
RB: Yes, but the cost to you, David. They want to know that.
NBP: Haha! Oh, Dick … Haha! You know that, too.
RB: But I can't tell them you're only paying €200 million but will own the €5 billion network after 25 years. They'll lynch me back home. And the rest of us.

NBP: Look, it's a tough sell and there may be another tribunal, but sure, we'll all have made enough money by then to surf through it. Denis, too.
RB: Ah for fuck sake, David. Just tell them the cost. We've faces to save here.
NBP: Don't worry, don't worry. You'll be out of office when the shit hits the proverbial fan at that stage and we can put you on the board for a nice fee. Keep your trap shut and plough on.
RB: Board wage? On top of my pension pot?
NBP: You know it, baby. Tell Leo and the lads that there'll be board jobs for them, too.
RB: Jesus, David. You're an awful man.
NBP: Haha! Sure, where would I be got?
RB: Haha! What will I tell these great unwashed? Jesus. There's an election brewing now, too.
NBP: I'm sure you crafty fuckers will think of something to distract them. Find a scandal on Sinn Féin or something.
RB: Look, go on ya scamp. Off with ya.
NBP: G'wan, Dick. I'll chat to you soon. It'll be grand. It's fucking Ireland – they'll take it like they always do.

CONVERSATION ENDS

TAOISEACH 'SURPRISED' TO HEAR HE HAS THE COMPETENCE LEVEL OF A PARAPLEGIC SLOTH

LEO Varadkar may be Taoiseach, but a new report into his current level of capabililty shows that he has the competence level of a paraplegic sloth, WWN can confirm.

The Taoiseach was one of several high-profile politicians who had their competence levels calculated as part of RTÉ's flagship politics show, *Operation Politician*, with Minister

for Health Simon Harris, Minister for Finance Paschal Donohoe, Minister for Transport Shane Ross and Tánaiste Simon Coveney also included.

'What is more interesting is that the majority of the ministers tested were even worse than Mr Varadkar, with Simon Harris coming in with the competence level of a squashed frozen pea stuck to the back of a thrown-out fridge-freezer,' read a section of the report detailing the results.

The relatively unsurprising report went on to classify Shane Ross as a 'lint particle clinging to a dying mongrel dog's nostril hair', with Paschal Donohoe performing the worst

out of the bad bunch, coming in with the competence level of a 'withering penis of a dried-up midge stuck to a Perspex motorcycle visor, in a recycle-bin container, headed on a slow boat to China'.

The report stated that its accuracy rates are within 0.00007 per cent, and concluded that the current state of the Irish government combined would be just too embarrassing to publish.

'We could go on, but I think the results speak for themselves already,' it summarised.

Animal facts

The white-tailed eagle was reintroduced to Ireland after a 200-year absence, stealing vital jobs from indigenous eagles.

DRUG wholesalers across the country have recalled €500 million worth of cocaine over fears the product may be contaminated with other substances, WWN has learned.

The Kinahan cartel apologised last night for the sudden recall, stating they had no other option, as traces of worm dose, baby powder and even dental painkillers were said to be found laced through their latest batch of cocaine.

'We are recalling 100 tonnes of our cocaine due to complaints from some of our valued customers both on street

KINAHAN CARTEL RECALLS 100 TONNES OF COCAINE OVER CONTAMINATION FEARS

and at wholesale level operating on the island of Ireland,' read an official statement from the multinational corporation today.

The move comes after a Dublin street dealer by the name of Decco Ryan discovered the contaminant while on the session, before breaking

out in a facial rash from what is believed to be baby powder – an agent Mr Ryan has been allergic to since a young age.

'I knew it was danced on de second I snorted it,' Ryan told reporters. 'Ya couldn't be selling that to people in good conscience, d'ya know wha' I mean?'

Underworld stocks in the cartel plummeted by 17 per cent during this morning's trading, but bounced back to finish just 3 per cent down on yesterday's closing bell after a new shipment arrived off the Spanish coast.

Meanwhile, the cartel's European operation has not been affected by the recall. 'Our operations in the UK, Holland, Spain, Italy, Morocco, Belgium, Eastern Europe, France and Germany will not be affected by this latest recall,' the statement read.

'The Kinahan cartel aims to continue bringing our European customers the finest quality, fair-trade cocaine from South America.'

UPDATE: Gardaí have issued a missing person alert for Decco Ryan, who has vanished from his home after originally reporting the contamination.

EXCLUSIVE

RESCUERS ATTEMPT TO FREE GEMMA O'DOHERTY, TRAPPED DOWN RABBIT HOLE

RESCUE services in Dublin were called to an undisclosed location this afternoon in an attempt to free a European election candidate who is believed to have become trapped down a very deep rabbit hole, WWN can confirm.

Anti-Corruption Ireland founder Gemma O'Doherty reportedly fell down the dangerous rabbit hole following a presidential bid last year, before eventually slipping deeper and deeper down the hole, which is understood to be surrounded by very dangerous terrain.

'There's all sorts of unusual and potentially damaging things down there that could harm Gemma and anyone else who might follow her,' one rescue worker explained.

'We're not sure whether there's toxic gases down there as she seems to be rambling on and on about very peculiar things that are not even worth mentioning here. It seems all logic and common sense has been left behind on the surface here.

'I don't think there's any hope of getting her back up to surface. She may have gone too far.'

O'Doherty, a once-brilliant investigative journalist and staff writer for the *Irish Independent*, is understood to have been joined by several other figures who are all believed to be in a similar situation, having fallen down the now-bottomless pit.

'From what we gather, Gemma, Jim Corr and a few other susceptible individuals were lured down the rabbit hole by conspiracy and alternative media websites. They have somehow crawled further into the abyss over the past few months, and are now so far down they cannot see the light of reality,' the rescuer added, trying to coax the group with hard facts. 'It's a pointless exercise at this stage. Either they've gone past the point of no return, or they see some kind of financial future in the hole and are just pretending to like it down there. I don't know.'

Since O'Doherty descended, thousands of followers have also made the journey down the rabbit hole, carrying wads of cash for O'Doherty and her peers. Rescuers believe the hole has now become a hazard and have called for the rabbit hole to be closed up before someone gets really hurt.

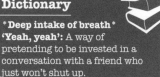

Suburban Dictionary

Deep intake of breath 'Yeah, yeah': A way of pretending to be invested in a conversation with a friend who just won't shut up.

PHOTO EXCLUSIVE

FINE GAEL AND FIANNA FÁIL CAUGHT HOLDING HANDS IN DÁIL CANTEEN

DESPITE insisting that the renewal of the Confidence and Supply deal is not a sign that the two parties are carbon copies of one another and yet further proof that they are taking the Irish public to the cleaners, Fianna Fáil and Fine Gael were caught lovingly holding hands underneath the table in the Dáil canteen at lunchtime.

Just hours after posturing on the steps outside the Dáil, and separately praising the new deal while highlighting that, really, the two parties are completely different and dislike each other intensely, FF and FG were busy scribbling each other's names into their notebooks, surrounded by hand-doodled hearts.

TDs not belonging to the two largest parties in the Dáil watched on aghast as the 49 TDs of Fine Gael brazenly canoodled with the 44 Fianna Fáil TDs while in the canteen, prompting Mary Lou McDonald to drop her lunch tray and proclaim 'The fuck is this? So you're not even hiding it any more?'

'Okay, so maybe, once upon a time, they didn't even talk to each other, but they've got that chemistry and sexual tension that can only come from a real sensual lust for power. They're mad about each other,' confirmed one onlooker, who had never seen such public displays of affection from power-hungry political parties before.

With the Confidence and Supply deal renewed, Fine Gael has been granted the opportunity to continue to ignore and underserve the marginalised, the poor and the hard-working but low-earning portions of the population.

'We couldn't have done it without you,' one Fine Gael member said to Fianna Fáil as their fingers caressed the hands of their fierce rivals, who have agreed to oppose nothing important.

'This is such squad goals. We're like Beyoncé and Jay-Z, or poverty and no State intervention. We just click so well, such a power couple,' added one Fianna Fáil member as she spoon-fed Fine Gael lasagna like it was the votes needed to stop any party other than Fine Gael passing a Bill.

Sources close to the loved-up parties suggest that a messy break-up is expected sometime in 2020, at which point everyone involved will claim they never even liked each other in the first place.

Community text alerts

There will be a support group meeting tonight for anyone currently being sued by Denis O'Brien. Standing room only.

ww news

Waterford Whispers News

LOCAL NEWS

LOCAL GIRL 'RUINED WITH TATTOOS'

A think-tank of esteemed Waterford gentlemen has emerged from a gruelling deliberation session during which time they ascertained that local girl Sheila Whelan used to be a lot better looking before she went and 'ruined herself' by getting a full sleeve tattoo done, as well as several other inkings around her person.

The cabal of predominantly single lads made their findings over pints in their local at the weekend, where they spotted Ms Whelan socialising with friends, prompting them to spend the rest of the night discussing the 'formerly attractive' 25-year-old, even though she hadn't given them so much as a passing glance.

'I'll tell you one thing, lads, we dodged a bullet there,' said Derek Sewell, who had a crush on Ms Whelan since school but wouldn't go near her now that she's destroyed herself with ink.

'Sure, what was she thinking? Going off and getting all them tattoos done, eh? Did she not consider what the lads in her locality find attractive, or did she just lose the run of herself altogether? It's an attention-seeking thing if you ask me, plus she probably

has, like, loads of other issues. That's not to mention what they'll look like when she's 50. Anyways, what are we at the rest of the night? Drinking our loneliness away? Fair enough.'

Meanwhile, Ms Whelan has yet to issue a statement on the matter, as she has a 'life to live and not a fuck to give'.

𝔚aterford 𝔚hispers News

Hitler 'invades' Poland, 1 September 1939

What we said then: A thoroughly vibrant personality, the world at large would benefit from more of his ilk. All these people giving out about the Kraut need to pipe down and respect German democracy. His remarks about the total obliteration of the Jewish people aside, he's a breath of fresh air and we can't just call for people with different views to be dismissed by society.

What we say now: Admittedly, we haven't gotten everything right during WWN's otherwise illustrious history, but I don't think anyone would dispute the fact that when you analyse the discourse at the time, there simply wasn't anyone out there suggesting Hitler was a wrong'un.

HEALTH

LOCAL GOOD-FOR-NOTHING IMMIGRANT SAVES LIVES AS SURGEON IN HOSPITAL

LOCAL social media was abuzz with yet another example of a local good-for-nothing immigrant poisoning the sacred soil of Mother Éire with his continued draining presence.

Outrage was first sparked this morning after a local radio programme showcasing yet again the reprehensible PC-gone-mad culture that Ireland has been swamped in, claiming that 44-year-old Pakistani national Dalir Eshan continues to shake Ireland down and take her to the cleaners.

'Can you believe we're paying for this?' confirmed irate radio host Michael Toland, informing his informed listeners of the cardiothoracic surgeon who spends his days saving the lives of people in Ireland.

'Who knows how long he's been getting away with it and they're all laughing at us,' he added, not going into any further detail about what was gotten away with,

who 'us' was, and who exactly was laughing at them and for what.

'PC gone mad …' Toland scoffed, who makes a tidy living from pretending to care about things.

Eshan is believed to be one of countless immigrants currently in Ireland, shamelessly filling skills shortages and, as unbelievable as it sounds, accepting payment for his specialist skill.

'I can't get any work,' explained one caller to Toland's *Hot Air Hour* show. 'It's them like your man with the funny name I can't pronounce that gets all the jobs I'd be happy to do,' he added, even though he is not a qualified cardiothoracic surgeon.

The phone-in show took a turn for the despicable when one caller rang in to claim 'Immigrants are human beings too,' forcing Toland to make an on-air apology to listeners affected by the unsavoury language used.

Bill's Campaign Diary

Veteran journalist Bill Badbody takes a leave of absence from his day-to-day reporting at WWN HQ to pursue a career in politics, in the hope of securing a place as MEP in the European elections. This is his story.

Week 3

Woke up late. Missed nurses' strike. Another strike? Bloody leeches. Fiachra went to a photo shop? Managed to put a picture of me beside the nurses, outside the hospital, like I was there. Amazing what they can do with technology these days!

Over 300 jobs announced in Waterford today. Pulled the old John Halligan trick, sharing the news and claiming the credit. Political stuff is fairly straightforward once you know all the tricks.

Kissed some people's babies for some photos today. Think I may have caught something. Probably that working-class kid with the wonky eye. Googled 'Is rickets contagious? Should be fine. The more ordinary Irish people I meet, the more I realise they don't want sensible long-term policies. They just want to give out about the foreigners, which is perfect for me because that is my only policy, really.

It's hard being away from home. I call Anne every day now on the phone, but she's so busy trying to get fit in time for when I'm elected. She'll look great beside me. Chatted last night and she was so out of breath her trainer Javier answered her phone. Actually, must ask Sergeant Roche to vet him.

Officially announced my proposal to ban all farm machinery from Irish roads. Amazed at the response and the support I received in the comments and personal messages. Even the farmers were blackguarding, saying they were going to come to my house and shoot me! A right gallery altogether. Cyclists next? Tax, insure them? NCT for bikes?

Woke up to the whole house and my two cars covered in what appears to be slurry! Called the gardaí. Wouldn't even hold the water hose when I was trying to wash down the Porsche and Audi. The EU are probably in on it with the farmers, funding the attack. I will not be silenced!

TRANSPORT

DOUBLE-DECKER LUAS GETS GO-AHEAD

IN response to the continued overcrowding on Luas trams during rush hour, Transport for Ireland has given the green light to a new double-decker-sized tram, WWN can reveal.

Stressed-out commuters have routinely complained about being packed into trams like sardines in a tin, except with worse-smelling people. Despite the introduction of longer Luas trams, there is no alternative but to build up and add a second floor to the transport system.

'Commuters constantly found trams to be jam-packed upon arriving at their stops and, as a result, there was no room for them. It would result in them being late for work,' confirmed Minister for Transport and Getting Sportspeople's Names Wrong Shane Ross.

In recent months, the situation had threatened to reach boiling point, as commuters glued themselves to the outside of trams. In some instances, commuters voluntarily removed several ribs from their rib cages, making it easier to contort themselves into the handful of small gaps left on trams at peak times.

'This additional floor on top of the Luas couldn't have come at a better time, given the time of year we're at now. Commuters will be delighted,'

> **'This additional floor on top of the Luas couldn't have come at a better time'**

added Ross, who noted that the new trams, with double the capacity, will also have double the amount of anti-social behaviour on them.

However, the 80 new trams, which cost €400 million in total, will not contain anywhere for Luas drivers to have their lunch.

A trial run of all 80 new trams this week has not gone according to plan, as commuters pointed out that the engineers behind the new double-decker trams had failed to install any stairs up to the second floor.

EXCLUSIVE

BIG BLUE KITCHEN ROLL STILL BEST THING FAMILY EVER BOUGHT

A 120-metre two-ply catering-sized blue kitchen roll may be the only thing keeping one Waterford family from tearing itself apart, after almost three full months of loyal service, during which time it has mopped up almost every fluid a human being can produce.

The Keenan family from Waterford city stand by their claim that the big blue kitchen roll remains the 'best €12 ever spent', after bringing home a six-pack of them from a shop that also sells massive boxes of Daz.

From Dad Martin's knocked-over cans of beer once he's fallen asleep on the couch after a few too many on a Saturday night, to the semen spilled by sixteen-year-old Seán after he's cracked one out under his covers, the big blue kitchen roll is right there with the family – a faithful, trusted friend in their hour of absorbent need.

'When we were buying expensive kitchen roll, you were always on a knife edge of tension when cleaning things up,' said mum Helen, wiping up a tiny spill with a huge fistful of blue roll.

'Like, you wanted your stuff to be dry, but you'd be trying to get the most out of each and every square of Bounty. But this blue roll? There's fucking miles of it! I don't even care when shit gets spilled around here anymore. We've got what it takes to cope with things like that. We've got a big blue roll that costs fucking cents per yard.

'Just the other day, my eldest son Derek got shot in the arm by a local drug gang as a warning for selling on their turf. He nearly bled to death in the hall because he didn't want to go to a doctor in case the cops found out. The place looked like Freddy Krueger's arsehole, but we just laughed throughout. The big blue roll cleaned the whole place down in minutes, then we took the kid to a vet.'

Mrs Keenan then just pissed on the floor, safe in the knowledge that she still had maybe 600 yards or so of big blue rolls left.

Animal facts

Birds have been strutting about like they own the place ever since they watched a BBC documentary about how they are descended from dinosaurs.

CLARE VOTED COUNTY MOST LIKELY TO MAKE A LOVELY SHOE

AFTER a survey of a map of Ireland and its counties, a carefully selected panel of Irish citizens has voted Clare the county most likely to make the loveliest-looking shoe.

As part of a government initiative tasked with squinting at maps and imagining real-world objects out of the shapes of individual counties, the 500-person panel overwhelmingly chose Clare when it came to the question of which one would make a nice kitten heel or casual boot you wouldn't wear when going 'out out'.

'We're not here to judge whether or not it would be comfortable to wear, just that it may or may not look like a lovely shoe,' head of the panel and former chief justice Noel Hingerty told WWN.

The vote has not been without opposition and criticism, however. Roscommon's tourism board lobbied heavily for their county to be chosen but, due to a technicality which means the rotation of a county is prohibited, Roscommon in its current orientation looks nothing like a shoe, let alone a lovely one.

'We'll fight this ruling and exhaust all our appeal options,' Roscommon County Shapes official Lenny Carmullen told WWN. 'It's madness. Just look at Roscommon, there. Now sit it on its side. If that's not a shoe then this isn't Ireland and there is no justice in the world.'

Being likened to a specific shape, and officially recognised as such, is worth a lot of money, with Clare now preparing itself for an influx of two million Japanese tourists in the coming weeks.

Killaloe

Ennis

West Clare

Shannon

RELATIONSHIPS

FRIENDS READY TO RIP INTO LOCAL WOMAN'S BOYFRIEND THE MINUTE SHE DUMPS HIM

A quartet of Waterford women are 'counting the days' until their pal, Sinéad, comes to her senses and dumps her current boyfriend, so they can unleash the eight months of stored-up hatred they have for him in one unmerciful bitching session.

Sinéad Haslan has been dating Eoghan Martin, known locally as a 'pure cunt', since February of this year, to the disgust of her pals, who all think he's, at best, a 'wanker' and, at worst, a 'total fucking wanker'.

With cracks beginning to show in the relationship, group spokeswoman Deirdre Whelan spoke exclusively to WWN about the shitshow that will go down the weekend after Sinéad wises up and dumps Eoghan.

'All of us hated that prick the minute we met him'

'We're not going to lie, we've had these punches cocked for months,' said Deirdre, just itching to take her pal out and get her locked.

'All of us hated that prick the minute we met him, and he's just gotten worse since then. It'll be the standard 'You're better than him' crying session to begin with, purely for show. Then it'll be into town in all our finery

for cocktails and making a show of ourselves, big kebabs, rip into Eoghan some more, then ride the next thing that comes along.'

The plan also includes an intensive six months of aftercare, to make sure Sinéad doesn't go back to Eoghan for the ride when she's lonesome on a Saturday night.

Animal facts

The hedgehog isn't the only prickly hog native to Ireland. There is the tree-hog, which resides in trees, and the Lidl-hog, which hangs out in bins at the back of Lidl stores.

FITNESS

LOCAL GIRL 'VERY DONE UP' FOR GYM

SEVERAL of the male patrons at a Waterford fitness centre have remarked on the overly made-up appearance of one of the gym's female customers, adding that she dresses in a provocative manner designed solely to distract lads who just want to lift weights, make gains and take selfies.

Putting aside the possibility that the as-yet-unnamed young lady may simply be attempting to do her own workout routine, without giving any thought whatsoever to anyone else in the gym, numerous men at Total Super Fitness are of the unshakeable belief

that this woman is some sort of 'fitness siren', attending the gym to flirt and show off.

As the young woman entered her second hour of free weights, and the young men entered their second hour of gawking at her, WWN asked one of the gym-top-wearing lads to walk us through what they felt was at play here.

'Well, she's very made up for the gym, isn't she? Make-up on, hair done, the works,' said one lad wearing runners but no socks, seemingly blind to the fact that the girl had minimal make-up on, and having her hair in a

ponytail hardly constituted having her 'hair done'.

'Nobody minds girls in the gym but, like, this is a place to work out. It's not a nightclub. And, yeah, I could be on the treadmill right now and, yeah, I could be doing squats now, but instead I'm here keeping an eye on herself over there … and that's 100 per cent her fault.'

The woman then left the gym, seemingly oblivious that her careless womanhood caused such a distraction for everyone.

Health and fitness tip

When attending your first spinning class, make sure you projectile vomit only on the person in front you.

NATURE

MEMBERS of a local town council gathered today to issue an official statement confirming that yes, they are cutting down all the trees and, yes, it was their decision to make.

Speaking from a makeshift press-conference table normally reserved for cocktail sausages, the committee of four men and three women began by telling local press and townspeople to 'shut your fucking mouths and listen for one fucking second.'

'We cut down all the town's trees overnight when you were asleep,' began town councillor Tracey Hacket. 'We just don't like the trees any more, okay? They're stupid-looking cunts. And before you start complaining, they're fucking trees, they'll grow back.'

Asked whether there was any solid reason as to why all the town trees were quickly cut down in their entirety, without any consultation

'We just don't like the trees any more, okay? They're stupid-looking cunts'

COUNCIL CULLING TREES WHETHER YOU FUCKING LIKE IT OR NOT

with the people who lived there and appreciated them, council member Tom Stafford abruptly stood up.

'Leaves or something. Fucking roots,' he shouted, 'whatever you're having yourself. What are we, fucking botanists? We just cut them down. They're not even wild trees anyway. They were captive trees. You could say we set them free.

'Yeah, that's it. We set them free,' Stafford finished, now nodding in agreement with the rest of the panel, who seemed to congratulate him on his stunning improvisation.

'I heard it was for 5G,' one local, long-haired man shouted up from the back of the unimpressed crowd to the panel, then was quickly silenced by a man with a chloroform-soaked cloth. 'The trees

stop mmhhff ... It's mind control mmhhff ...' he tried to add, before falling limp to the ground and being dragged out of the community hall.

'Any other fucking questions?' another stern-looking female council member asked, pointing at the meek crowd in an intimidating fashion. 'No? Good. Meeting adjourned.'

Suburban Dictionary

'What's for you won't pass you': A blatant lie people tell others after they've received bad news or misfortune has visited them, such as failing the Leaving Cert, being broken up with, or having their mickey torn clean off in a workplace accident.

WEDDINGS

CHEAPSKATE COUPLE TO HAVE 'INTIMATE WEDDING'

RATHER than throw what they call a 'vulgar, ostentatious display of excess' for their upcoming nuptials, Waterford couple Eileen Sheridan and Cathal McFarrell have opted for what they describe as a 'serene, intimate ceremony', which has nothing to do with the fact they have a strict budget and they're fucked if they go over it.

'We don't need all the bells and whistles. We just need a priest, my folks, her folks, and maybe, like, thirty other people,' said McFarrell, going through Google for the cheapest florist he could find because they're 'only going to get thrown out the next day'.

'You see these huge weddings with all the friends and all the family … Do you really need that? Wouldn't it be better if there were just a few people there, to really share in what me and my fiancée are coming together in? And, also, wouldn't it be a bonus if this thing cost three grand, tops?'

Although most women would love a big fairy-tale wedding, Eileen Sheridan shares her husband-to-be's penny-wise attitude to the big day.

'What's the best part of any wedding? The cocktail sausages, right?' she beamed, buying her dress on AliExpress.

'Why not just have them for dinner? Forget beef or salmon. Cocktail sausages. I'll do them myself in the fryer when we get out of the chapel and head back to the house, before Cathal gets the Spotify playlist going. It's exactly the type of intimate wedding we've always dreamed of!'

Sheridan and McFarrell also hinted that they'd still like at least 200 quid from each guest as a gift, specifying this in the WhatsApp wedding invitations they sent round.

Health and fitness tip

Purchasing a specially designed ab roller can help you lose as much as €50 in one day.

LOCAL MAN IS GRAND, TAKE YOUR FUCKING HANDS OFF HIM

LOCAL man Gareth Whelan doesn't need any help getting home. He's just out for a few drinks. You don't need to ring anyone. He's grand. Just leave him be and go on about your business. Sure, he's only enjoying himself, WWN can report.

Whelan, 26, will go home when he's ready. Would you ever fuck off and stop annoying him? You mind your business and he'll mind his. No, you don't need to ring anyone to come get him. He's not bothering anyone. Now, are you going to serve him another drink or does he have to go elsewhere?

Local man Whelan just wants you to look the other way. Don't be looking over here at him. You look over there and mind your fucking business. He means it, now. Quit looking at him like that, alright? Listen, get your fucking hands off him. He's warning you, now. Don't fucking start. What's your fucking problem, anyway?

'Get your hands off me,' said Whelan, who was grand, not a bother on him.

'Get … get the … get your fuckin' hands off me. Go away the fuck. I'm fuckin' warning you, lad. Don't start. I'm grand. I've only had a few drinks. I'm grand. You just … fucking … you, take your fuckin' hands off me now. I'm telling you this, take your fuckin' hands off me.'

AWARDS

GQ MEN OF THE YEAR AWARDS SNUBS DAD WHO CHANGED SHITTY NAPPY WITHOUT WAKING BABY

ONCE again, the *GQ* Men of The Year Awards have managed to completely snub the true shining examples of manliness in this world, including father-of-one Declan Jennings, who carried off the save of the century in March, when he changed his infant son's pooey nappy without waking the child up from the first big sleep he'd had in nearly a month.

The Waterford father-of-one had eagerly awaited a nomination in the category of 'International Man of the Year', believing his achievements to be up there with anything from the arts, sports or entertainment worlds – a once-in-a-lifetime victory that should stand as an inspiration to fathers around the globe.

'Chadwick Boseman … International Man of the Year … Chad, I liked *Black Panther*, but let's see you wet-wipe Weetabix out of a child's arse without waking him up,' fumed Jennings, whose wife Keeley had showered him with praise for saving their precious night in front of the telly with his skills.

'And look at this lad over here, this fucking Jonathan Yeo chap, a painter

… he's Painter of the Year? I painted that nursery in there. You'd want to have seen the state of it when I got to it first. Now look at it. I drew that Tigger in there by hand. Hi, Yeo, paint me a Tigger with a 4-inch roller set from Woodies. Then tell me you're better than me.'

Jennings was not alone on the snub list, which had instead awarded stars such as Harry Kane, Sacha Baron Cohen and Johnny Marr over men like Will Hanlon, who scored a cracking goal to secure victory for his work team Oughterard Meats United over their hated rivals Drews' Shoes FC at astro last Friday, or Dublin man Steve Finlay who, after five years of living with his girlfriend, finally learned the 'right way' to sit on the toilet.

Community text alerts

Recently deceased man Danny Sheehan was only spotted out shopping in the garden centre the other day. Looked fine then – bet it was the Roundup.

SCIENCE

YOUNG SCIENTIST OF THE YEAR METH LAB EXPOSED

'Thousands of kids enter each year, and we're fairly certain that they're not all doing it for their love of Bunsen burners'

QUESTIONS are being raised about the future of the BT Young Scientist of the Year Award after a special undercover garda unit discovered a sophisticated crystal-meth lab in a Waterford secondary school.

Seventeen students from Our Lady of the Odd Labia were arrested in the dawn raid, along with a seizure

of €100,000 worth of the highly addictive drug, manufactured under the guise of a Young Scientist project on 'climate change or something'.

With evidence mounting that the school had been supplying the entire county with meth for years, gardaí have ordered a halt on any further Young Scientist activity in schools while they ascertain if any more labs exist in the country.

'Applications for BT YSOTY 2020 are now on hold,' said Sergeant Derek Hamlin, holding a bag of meth in one hand and a student by the ear in the other.

'Thousands of kids enter each year, and we're fairly certain that they're not all doing it for their love of Bunsen burners. We've got operatives acting as kids in schools across the country, sort of a *21 Jump Street* thing, and we're closing in on an LSD plant in Macroom as we speak.'

People are being warned to watch out for any student who claims to be working on a Young Scientist project, particularly if they drive to school in a 191 white Audi.

Fullmindness

Breathing exercises are important. Start by going all 'puff, puff, puff' really quickly for, like, ten minutes.

EDUCATION

'IT'S THE WAY IT'S TAUGHT,' CONFIRMS MAN WHO DIDN'T DO A TAP IN IRISH CLASS

DESPITE attending formal education from the age of four until the age of 18, one Waterford man continues to point the finger of blame for his failure to retain any Irish whatsoever at the way the language is taught.

While hardworking former students with a high aptitude for learning often bemoan the way Irish is taught in schools, Tramore native Martin Bohan has used the same reasoning for his poor understanding of Irish, even though it was because he never did a tap of work for 14 years.

'Ah, the way it's taught is a disgrace. Ye haven't a hope of mastering it, even if you were dying to learn like I was,'

Bohan remarked, placing himself in the large group of Irish people who tried hard to learn Irish but never quite carried it with them after leaving school.

However, when WWN delved into Mr Bohan's past, his tale of focus and dedication to the *cúpla focail* fell apart.

'Is that the same Martin Bohan who was rushed to hospital in the middle of the Leaving Cert Irish aural because he somehow managed to stuff 14 HB pencils into his nostrils, that Martin Bohan?' queried one former classmate of Bohan's, one of about a dozen people who confirmed he wouldn't

be appearing on *Mastermind* anytime soon.

'It's the way it's taught. Honestly, it's dreadful. And there was me, willing to put in the work and do me homework. I was let down, so I was. Anyway, thanks for interviewing me, or should I say "Griff-meals-a-moths-in-guts, *slán*",' confirmed Bohan.

DONEGAL MAN'S SNORING REGISTERS 2.1 ON THE RICHTER SCALE

A minor earthquake recorded in County Donegal last night is thought to have been caused by the vibration of respiratory structures belonging to local man Thomas Dooley, investigators confirmed today.

The 2.1 magnitude quake, which struck at 9.18 p.m. last night, was sourced to the house of Mr Dooley, about 15 kilometres southeast of Donegal Town. There, his wife Sharon Dooley confirmed that it was her husband's snoring which registered on the scale, and not an actual earthquake.

'Same thing happened a few weeks ago,' Mrs Dooley explained, referring to a similar earthquake reported on 7 April. 'Every time he goes down to play cards, he comes back twisted drunk and ends up sleeping on his back on the floor. He keeps the whole

neighbourhood awake, and now this – making front-page news – it's so embarrassing.'

Following some date-checking, it is believed Mr Dooley has been responsible for just about every tremor in the region for the past 20 years, with his wife vowing to bring him to the doctor about it.

'We tried everything, including a snoring ring, special pillows and even Sellotaping a football to his fat back so he sleeps on his side. Nothing will stop his nose flaps from vibrating,' his exhausted wife added. 'I'm driven demented.'

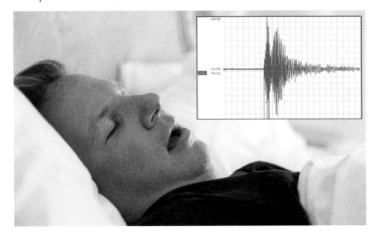

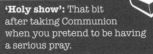

Suburban Dictionary

'Holy show': That bit after taking Communion when you pretend to be having a serious pray.

COUNTY KERRY: IRELAND'S AREA 51?

THE government has finally come clean and admitted that the county known as Kerry was originally Ireland's answer to Area 51.

Thanks to a Freedom of Information Request made by WWN, we were able to force the government into conceding that Kerry was the area of the country exclusively reserved for controversial high-tech government and military experimentation, which explains a lot.

'The phrase "There's something in the water down there" is actually

just a true statement when it comes to Kerry. We spiked the water. As an experiment, the result of which was Kerry,' explained retired Irish army scientist Dr Helmut Schneer.

Schneer was tasked with concocting all manner of ghastly experiments during the 1920s, 30s and 40s on the flora and fauna in the fenced-off land most people know today as Kerry, mainly in a bid to arm Ireland with effective weaponry in the event Britain ever sought to invade Ireland again.

'My most regrettable experiment, Swamp Man, involved mating a wild pig with an even wilder pig, and then mating that pig with an alien who crash-landed to Earth from a planet obsessed with tarmacking roads and necking pints. I infused turf and Guinness into its blood-

stream,' recalled Schneer. 'He grew too powerful and broke out of his restraints, never to be seen again. But what I do know is much of Kerry is now populated with his direct descendants.'

'There was a constant trail of vans that used to go into that place at all hours. Big vans with vats of neon-looking liquids. Then there were the cages that had animals in them, the likes of which I'd never seen before,' revealed one Cork native who lived next door to the top-secret facility and county.

While the government has admitted the existence of experimentation on the area known as Kerry, and that they did indeed play God, and that it was a mistake, there is little sign they will issue an apology on behalf of the State.

BANKING

AIB UNVEIL NEW ARMED ATM 3000

IRISH banking institution AIB has today unveiled a brand new, heavily armed ATM robot, which they say will combat a spate of robberies that have plagued banks around the country.

The new ATM 3000 comes equipped with a .50 calibre automatic assault cannon, which can pierce through thick, reinforced steel, and even JCB shovels, due to be launched nationwide early next week.

Community text alerts

Just a reminder that Saturday is set to be a scorcher, so the good-looking Eastern European in number 19 will almost certainly be lying out the front of the house again.

'Following some minor glitches in lab testing, we've finally managed to sign off on this new armed ATM, and look forward to seeing it in action,' AIB spokesman Jonathan Holden told a congregation of press and photographers outside a Galway branch earlier today, after unveiling the bank's latest security measure.

In trial tests, however, subjects wearing headgear triggered the ATM 3000's sensors into combat mode and were accidentally obliterated by the robot, forcing the bank to issue a warning for customers wishing to use the new machines.

'Unfortunately, there will be teething problems until people realise that if they don't take off their helmets or headgear, they will end up as steaming piles of human mince.

'If they don't take off their helmets or headgear, they will end up as steaming piles of human mince'

There will be plenty of signs to remind customers of this, so this little glitch shouldn't be a problem,' he continued.

As part of the new security measures, the new ATM will also engage subjects who input their PIN incorrectly three times, thus acting as a deterrent to criminals trying to use stolen cards.

'We don't predict any issues with this new armed ATM,' the AIB spokesperson concluded.

EXCLUSIVE

LOCAL MAN FALSELY CLAIMING HE'S OVER SIX FEET TALL

ONE Waterford man has hit new heights when it comes to maintaining a long-standing lie, no matter the circumstances, as he continues to falsely claim he is over six feet tall.

Declan Toland, 34, has maintained the lie that he is six-foot-two for close to 16 years now, and an investigation carried out by WWN suggests there is no sign of him coming clean any time soon.

'About six-foot-two,' Toland has most frequently and casually stated when asked what his height is, in the belief that women are much more impressed by a more elongated man. The Dungarvan-based painter and decorator settled on six-foot-two as

his completely made-up height after deciding that if he said he was just one inch above the six-foot barrier, people would become suspicious.

He also maintains a near-encyclopaedic knowledge of famous people who are six-foot-two, so he can let people know he is the same height as them if they ever come up in conversation.

Increasingly finding ways to bring his superior height into conversation when around women he wants to impress, Toland, who is single, is so far down the rabbit hole of his lie that he is no longer aware of his actual, real height.

'Declan, bless him, he's about five-foot-ten, I'd say. No harm in it. In fact, it's above average. I'm six-foot-two, and there's an obvious enough difference in height between us. But when I broached it with him once, he got very touchy,' confirmed Toland's long-time friend Gary Custerly.

In a bid to maintain the lie he lives, Toland is careful to never stand back to back with Custerly and has promised himself he will immediately leave a room if it has a measuring tape in it.

Suburban Dictionary

'If he had brains he'd be dangerous': Refers to someone of superior intellect, who has such a gifted way of looking at things, they are certain to change the world for the better.

WWN Was There

𝔚aterford 𝔚hispers News

The end of World War II, 2 September 1945

What we said then: Aw, really? Just when things were getting exciting.

What we say now: Saying war is 'exciting' is not an endorsement of the killing of millions, it's just a verifiable scientific fact.

BREAKING NEWS

IRA RELEASE OFFICIAL STATEMENT ON TOILET DOOR OF PUB

IN a week of high tensions and uncertainty surrounding Brexit and how it will affect the Irish border with Northern Ireland, the Irish Republican Army (IRA) has issued a worrying new statement this week, on a toilet door of a well-known Dublin pub, WWN can confirm.

Using what appears to be a permanent black marker, a spokesman for the paramilitary organisation penned a chilling but short note on the

> ### 'They're obviously very well trained and were in and out in a flash'

back of a cubicle door in the gents' bathroom of the Canary House bar in south Dublin.

The warning, which read 'IRA 2018. We haven't gone away!', was spotted by a surprised customer last Sunday evening, shortly after he sat down to empty his bowels.

'I'd say I just missed them by seconds,' recalls a Canary House regular, who wished to remain anonymous. 'I had no idea they were still around, to tell you the truth. I thought they had gone away.'

Staff at the bar reported the find to gardaí, and an armed response unit was deployed to the bar for fear the IRA might be hiding somewhere on the premises.

'You'd think you'd spot a group of men wearing camouflage and balaclavas going in and out of the jacks,' barman Conor Walsh told WWN, 'but none of us here saw anything like that.

'They're obviously very well trained and were in and out in a flash.'

The eerie statement, which looms over various other statements about penis sizes and how bad Liverpool FC are, is one of hundreds of similar IRA messages left by the organisation in Irish bars, raising fears over the current Brexit negotiations.

'This obvious threat to peace could break down talks about a hard border with the UK,' Taoiseach Leo Varadkar pointed out, after visiting the toilet earlier today.

Meanwhile, Sinn Féin have since rubbished the find, stating it was probably written by members of the UVF trying to reignite tensions in the North.

SHOCK AS DUBLIN RENTAL FOUND TO BE MADE ENTIRELY FROM LEGO

DUBLIN city landlords have come under fire yet again following the discovery of a rented-out semi-detached home, which was entirely constructed from old Lego bricks, WWN can confirm.

James Casey, 56, had been four months into his €1890-per-month lease on the three-bedroom home when he discovered brightly coloured plastic bricks after scratching what he thought was a legitimate wall while moving furniture.

'I was pulling the chair closer to the wall when I hit its wooden arm off the wallpaper,' Casey told a local radio station this morning. 'It made an odd sound, so I looked, and lo and behold there were Lego bricks underneath it.'

Fearing for his safety, Casey contacted the local gardaí to question the homeowner.

Following further investigation, the landlord admitted to collecting rent for 16 other dwellings in the city, which are also constructed using questionable building materials, including Meccano, straw bales, and even one house made entirely from Bord na Móna briquettes.

'We believe he targeted empty end-of-terrace properties, where there was no neighbour, and illegally built onto the side of them unnoticed,' a garda source confirmed. 'He was making 50 grand a week and we think this is just the tip of the iceberg in Dublin.'

Health and fitness tip

Eating five kilos of kale a day is key to turning your urine green.

NUTRITION

LOCAL MAN IS A DIVIL FOR THE BISCUITS

WHETHER it be Residents' Association meetings, parent–teacher meetings, wakes, funerals, baptisms, business meetings or forest raves, no matter what the occasion, if it serves up complimentary biscuits, local man John Davitt will stop at nothing to consume them all.

Davitt spoke candidly to WWN about his struggle with never once in his life managing to gather enough strength to say no to the offer of some biscuits.

'You might pop into a friend's house and have a cup of tea, share a chat, and then the inevitable biscuit offer comes along. You can say no, but I just ... I can't,' Davitt shared, before going to describe his life of biscuit-consuming carnage.

During a particularly dark chapter in Davitt's life, he consumed an entire packet of rich-tea biscuits before realising he wasn't in his own home and that he had, in fact, broken into someone's house to make a cup of tea, just so he'd have an excuse to 'break out the biscuits'.

'The phrase "Break out the biscuits" or "Bring out the biscuits" is a big trigger for me. You say that out loud and I'll just somehow have my mouth filled with eight Mikados within 60 seconds. I don't know how I do it,' said Davitt who, true to his word, was stuffing his face with biscuits.

'Sometimes, I swear to God, I'll walk into a room and my body just pulls me to them. I might not have even seen any biscuits with my own eyes. It's like some sort of GPS.' The GPS Davitt speaks of is, of course, the well-known genetic mutation found in Irish people referred to as BLS, or Biscuit Locating System.

BREAKING NEWS

LOCAL WOMAN ENTERING 'LITTLE TARTAN TROLLEY PHASE' OF LIFE

WATERFORD woman Claire Looney is today taking stock of her life, after a pivotal road-to-Damascus moment in town earlier this morning when, laden down with groceries, she thought to herself, 'I must get myself one of those little tartan wheelie lads.'

Looney, 55, had been doing her mid-week shop – not her big shop, now – when her mind began to drift towards a solution to carrying her messages, purse, phone and any other accoutrements without buying a 'Bag for Life', which would inevitably get lost in the press full of bags, never to be seen again.

'I thought to myself, what if I had a little suitcase? Like when I'm going on holidays,' sighed Looney, who started listening to the deaths on the radio a few weeks back, first as a matter of habit, then as a matter of actual life and death.

'With a handle, so you can just pull it behind yourself, put your stuff in it, and that way you don't have to actually carry a bag of spuds and three litres of milk around with you. Then it hit me. I was thinking about how handy it would be to have a granny cart. A fucking granny cart! That's it, lads. That's me fucked.'

Since that fateful moment, Looney has found herself searching the Internet for what will be an inevitable purchase, having resigned herself to the fact that she is shifting into the 'tartan trolley phase' of her life.

'They're surprisingly hard to find,' mused Looney, who can feel a draft coming from somewhere.

'I'm not even sure what the fuck they're called. Nothing comes up when I Google "Sad old woman basket thing on wheels".'

Bill's Campaign Diary

Veteran journalist Bill Badbody takes a leave of absence from his day-to-day reporting at WWN HQ to pursue a career in politics, in the hope of securing a place as MEP in the European elections. This is his story.

Week 4

Spoke to a lovely woman called Gemma O'Doherty on the YouTube last night and was amazed by the amount of supportive comments she was getting and, more important, the large cash donations. Got Fiachra to set up a thing called PaidPal, where random people just send you money in exchange for telling them foreigners are the reason poor people are broke. All tax-free!

Barely recognised Anne when I got home this evening. Face red as a beetroot from working out in her lingerie, which was strange ... She said her gym clothes were too heavy and just wanted to look her best for me. Security lights went on outside the house and Rex started barking like crazy. Could Europe be spying on me? Going to get security cameras in the house, just to be safe.

Shopping at M&S earlier and spotted Muslim parked in a disabled spot. Reported him to the local gardaí. Even took a picture and tagged the Islamic Council of Ireland, who still haven't condemned the attack on disabled Irish people. A new low for Islam and, of course, Marks & Spencers.

Passed the church and noticed a huge funeral. Lucky had suit in car. Deceased was fairly well-respected, so showed my face. Must check for apps that notify politicians of local funerals. If none, get Fiachra to make one. He's great with computers. Also, must check why mass-goers are allowed to park illegally.

Sitting down after a hard day to find a film called *White Chicks* on Virgin Media One. Repulsive that it's acceptable to don 'whiteface' like that. When black people do it, it's called 'acting', but when I dress as Osama bin Barack Obama at the 2007 Indo Xmas party, I get kicked out of Fianna Fáil. Explain that to me!

Classifieds

Foreign Neighbour: I'm quite racist and like to give out about non-nationals taking valuable welfare benefits and social housing from good, honest, actually Irish people. Only problem is, I've never actually met these people. If you're from outside Ireland, could you move in to my estate and bring to life the nightmares that fuel my late-night rants on Twitter? Much appreciated.

Email me at proudsonofeireblacksout@gmail.com.

TRANSPORT

NAAS TO BE RELOCATED TO WEST OF IRELAND TO CURB DUBLIN TRAFFIC

AN Bord Pleanála has green-lighted a €30 billion proposal to relocate the entire town of Naas to the west of Ireland in a bid to curb the flow of traffic coming into Dublin city.

Naas, which is currently situated on the outskirts of Dublin and found to be the main congestion source for

the N7, will begin its move in January 2019, when some 21,000 residents are to be relocated to a rural site in County Mayo that's out of the way.

'I suppose it will be worth it if it stops all that nightmare traffic every morning and evening,' said Naas man Derek Roche. 'It will actually take me the same time to commute to Dublin from Mayo with the changes, so I don't really mind moving at all.

'It's a great idea and Mayo's a beautiful place, too. I don't think anyone in Naas will complain.'

For years, the satellite town has been cursed by commuters travelling to work in Dublin from major cities like Cork, Limerick, Waterford and

Kilkenny, with the town becoming more of a hindrance as the country's population soared.

'It's just in the way and has to go,' explained one Limerick commuter, whose car has two million miles on the clock. 'Getting out of Dublin is hard enough, but when you hit that bottleneck at Naas, you might as well just park up the car and sleep there until morning. It's a form of torture.'

It is understood the current site for Naas will be levelled and turned into a car park for Dublin, while ongoing road maintenance works will widen the N7 by six more lanes to cater for the only city in Ireland where there are decent-paying jobs.

Fullmindness

Focus only on the now. Put aside whatever horrible things you have done in the past to people, despite how hard and how long they scream for help in the background. Let their screams soothe you to sleep.

MEATH AND WESTMEATH MEET AT KINNEGAD FOR REUNIFICATION TALKS

DELEGATIONS from the warring counties of Meath and Westmeath descended on the border town of Kinnegad today, chosen as the venue for the first official reunification talks between the two entities.

The People's Republic of Proper Meath and the Sovereign Socialist Republic County of Westmeath arrived at the demilitarised zone of the Tesco's car park, bidding to end a conflict which began centuries ago and claimed the lives of all inhabitants of north and south Meath.

'They should be Eastmeath if we're calling ourselves Westmeath. They think they're so great because they're "*Meath* Meath",' confirmed one delegate, whose grandfather's grandfather fought in the historic battles known as the 'Great Schemozzle' in Slane, and the '2 a.m. Skirmish at Supermac's' in Athlone.

> **'They should be Eastmeath if we're calling ourselves Westmeath. They think they're so great because they're "*Meath* Meath"'**

On the table for discussion is the reunification of families from both counties, the banishment of all blow-ins from Dublin, and the possibility of combining GAA teams, although Meath seems reluctant to do so.

'This historic meeting could herald much-needed progress. We continue to offer our support,' confirmed UN mediators, who were on scene, helping with the aid of translators.

Prominent figures from both counties were present to lend their support to reunification, including Pierce Brosnan, Niall Horan, Robbie Henshaw, Trevor Giles and a reanimated Joe Dolan. Hector Ó hEochagáin attempted to gain entry but was taken out by Meath's own snipers.

Long cut off from one another, and with no indication of how the other side lives, Meath brought pictures of their way of life, which consisted only of Tayto Park, while Westmeath delegates brought pictures of a flooded Athlone.

Health and fitness tip

Resting in between workouts is important, but make sure your rest period is no greater than five years.

TRAVEL GUIDE

WHAT'S IT LIKE TO BE FROM CORK?

PEOPLE from Cork are often referred to as arrogant and insufferable pricks who would win every Olympic gold medal if ignorance and bluster was a sporting event.

Harmless observations aside, the question remains: is this true? What are people from Cork really like? What is it like to hail from the Rebel County, the place those irritating langers refer to as the 'People's Republic'?

WWN, in a bid to either prove or disprove the good-natured jibes about people from Cork being complete and utter bastards, went undercover.

Unbeknownst to a young Cork couple, we smuggled ourselves into the womb of one Deirdre Hinglety. She gave birth to us nine months later and, from there, we posed as her and her husband Michael's child. (If you think this involved placing ourselves inside a condom, poking holes in it and fertilising an egg, you are only 46 per cent correct.)

Now, 'technically', we were born in Cork, to Cork parents. We were, as the county's Cork Supremacists call it, 'pure Cork'.

All that was left now was to immerse ourselves in our Corkness: grow up in Cork, go to school in Cork – live, eat, breathe Cork. Only then would we be able to report with full authority on what it was like to be from Cork.

Soon, the seemingly 'unknowable' became known. Living daily in Cork, talking to people from Cork, discussing Cork things, we began to get a feeling for the essence of Corkness.

Some 27 years after posing as Deirdre and Michael's unusually large and articulate newborn child with a heavy Waterford accent, we can report that being from Cork isn't just a case of being arrogant, anti-Dublin and anti-everywhere-else.

How foolish and ignorant we had been. It was a lot more sinister than that. Infinitely so. What do people from Cork do when no one's looking? For the first time, we have the shocking, stomach-turning facts.

Sure, it looks like they maintain a life largely similar to everyone else in the country. They have roads, schools, shops, sports teams and so on.

But they're preparing for a war, folks.

Every morning in Cork schools, when they're sure no non-Cork heads are watching, the blackboards are flipped to reveal endless Cork propaganda etched in chalk.

We were marched in formation in school yards and warned to prepare for 'Judgement Day'. This is done with every citizen of Cork from the age of four.

Judgement Day is, of course, when Corkonians will rise up and seal off the county from outsiders, declaring independence.

Gathering 27 years' worth of counter-intelligence, we left behind Deirdre and Michael, who we had become quite attached to, it must be said, and we presented our findings to An Garda Síochána up in Dublin.

As a senior garda poured over the undeniable facts of a genocidal plan aimed at eradicating everyone in Ireland not from Cork, the garda asked us to wait in a cell as his eyes turned red, which, upon reflection, we should have seen as a bad sign.

We waited patiently when, suddenly, the cell door opened and there they were: Simon Coveney, Roy Keane, Diarmuid 'The Rock' O'Sullivan, Anna Geary, the ghost of Jack Lynch, Sonia O'Sullivan, Cillian Murphy and Dáithí Ó Sé.

'What are you doing here, Ó Sé? You're from fucking Kerry,' we asked, a bit confused.

'Shut up! You think I'm gonna side with the losers in this war?' he responded, which is fair enough.

Suddenly, their eyes all turned a bright, incandescent shade of red.

'Forget what you've fucking seen,' they all said in unison.

So yeah, in summary: being from Cork is grand and there's nothing sinister going on. We can all sleep soundly tonight.

MOTORING

LOCAL MAN PROUD FOR ALLOWING FOREIGN NATIONAL CROSS AT PEDESTRIAN CROSSING

A County Waterford motorist said he was fairly chuffed with his own behaviour today, after stopping his car at a pedestrian crossing to let a foreign national cross the road like a normal person.

Joe Price described the moment as 'groundbreaking', stating that he could see the Muslim woman's eyes were full of gratitude as he waved her across the road in her long black hijab.

'Sure, they have to live, too,' Price told WWN, while recalling the international incident on the Manor Road, where a new orange-lighted pedestrian crossing was recently erected. 'I spotted her in the corner of my eye and I immediately knew she wasn't Irish, so I made an extra effort to put on that nice face I'd normally save for young children, and I even smiled as I instructed her to cross the road.'

Mr Price believes the mutual understanding of the rules of the road and common courtesy were both reached at the defining moment, and that the woman probably has a totally different outlook on Irish people thanks to his really kind gesture.

'I'm sure she spent the whole day telling everyone how nice I was to stop in such a welcoming way,' Price concluded. 'Hopefully she doesn't get in trouble with her husband for engaging with her eyes like that. I wouldn't like her to get beaten for something so pure and innocent. You know how them lads are.'

Suburban Dictionary

'Sneaky pint?': A harmless invitation to partake in endless drinking, which ends up with you being caught on CCTV at 3 a.m. soiling yourself and your family's good name.

WOMAN GOING ON ABOUT GIVING BIRTH LIKE IT WAS GETTING KICKED IN THE BALLS OR SOMETHING

THE incessant prattling on about childbirth by one Waterford woman is beginning to grate on nearby men as she continues to insist the pain she experienced comes close to the excruciating ordeal that is getting kicked in the testicles.

Sarah Mulcahy, hard to take at the best of times, has roused the irritation of her male friends by regaling them with an exaggerated account of labour in which she erroneously puts her pain on a par with what's felt by men being struck in the gonads.

'Where does she get off? Have you ever heard such insensitive, sexist nonsense in your life?' queried one of Mulcahy's friends, John, who could only scoff incredulously as the mother-of-three showed no signs of shutting up.

'And then I was basically ripped from here to here. It was like a horror movie on speed, I kid you not,' Mulcahy continued, failing to identify the anger in the eyes of her friends, who just could not believe what they were hearing.

'God, imagine going through that,' remarked another of the Mulcahy's male friends, Tom. 'Really, imagine what she went through for 23 hours and to have the gall to then equate it to the hell we go through when we get a flick, punch, kick or thump to the bollocks. The neck of her, honestly.'

Mulcahy's comments join a long list from women who continue to go unchallenged when they engage in over-the-top female bravado boasting sessions.

TRAVEL

TOURISM BOARD AGREES TO JUST NOT MENTION THE MIDLANDS

WITH more tourists flocking to Ireland than at any other time in the past decade, Tourism Ireland has commended itself for initiatives such as the Wild Atlantic Way and Ireland's Ancient East, while at the same time quietly shelving plans to 'do something' with the Midlands.

Although the vast majority of Ireland is made up of non-coastal territory, the tourism board has struggled to come up with a compelling reason to visit any of it. While Mullingar has occasionally been referred to as the 'passage to the West', it really just means the bypass.

After throwing around a few ideas such as the 'Soggy Middle' and 'All This Shit', Tourism Ireland has decided it's probably best to double down on the edges of the country and just brush over everything else.

'The North has *Game of Thrones*. The Midlands has what, Vikings? We can't fucking sell Vikings,' said a spokesperson for TI, before concluding, 'Nah, we'll stick with the coasts. The Sunny South East is gorgeous. The Skelligs sell themselves. What are we going to do? Put up a poster in the airport of a fight outside a Supermac's in Belturbet to greet tourists as they arrive?'

EXCLUSIVE

NATION SO RACIST ASYLUM HOTELS SPONTANEOUSLY COMBUST OF OWN ACCORD

FIRE forensic teams investigating a series of fires at hotels earmarked to house asylum seekers in Ireland have concluded that the buildings spontaneously combusted of their own accord, WWN can confirm.

Investigators believe that the fires were not started by any one individual, but were due to a national accumulation of racism which has festered in the country over the past five years. 'Both fires seemed to have just started by themselves. We believe the cause to be a form of pyrokinesis,' explained arson investigator Darren Tobin.

Pyrokinesis is the purported psychic ability that allows people to create and control fire with their minds. It is understood that when large groups of people filled with hate and ignorance want something badly enough, it can manifest into a destructive force like fire, and destroy a target within minutes.

'We believe that such is the racism in Ireland that both hotels in Donegal and Leitrim spontaneously combusted under the mental kinetic energy of the surrounding racists, sending the properties into flames,' Tobin added. 'All you have to do is check out any comment section on any article about these two incidents to realise the level of racism in this country.'

Ireland's underlying racism began floating to the surface during the recession, thanks to the rise in right-wing online propaganda which fed into the nation's deep-seated hatred for immigration, whilst conveniently forgetting its own mass emigration in the same period.

'They say the reason people hate others is set in the fact that they see something in someone else that reminds them of their old selves,' one expert concluded. 'But, to be honest, I think it's really just down to the large number of thick, ignorant cunts living here.'

CHILDCARE

NEW CRÈCHE SCHEME WILL SEE TODDLERS WORK FOR THEIR CHILDCARE

A government scheme aimed at cutting the punishing cost of childcare will see toddlers and infants put to work at adorable little assembly lines, cutting their crèche fees by up to 50 per cent, if they're very good little boys and girls.

More than 500 crèches and Montessori schools around the country have participated in trial runs of the scheme, which has seen kids as young as six months perform simple tasks such as component sorting, chicken sexing, and small jewellery construction, easing their parents' childcare bills to the point where it actually

doesn't seem like such a waste of time staying in work.

The scheme is set to roll out to all crèches on a purely voluntary basis, with parents perfectly within their rights to keep their child out of the 'chain babies' programme if they don't mind paying a second mortgage every month just for the privilege of leaving their heartbroken kids with a stranger for every waking hour of their lives.

'I mean, I'd rather he wasn't threading beads onto necklaces for seven hours a day while I stare at his picture on my desktop in a job that I hate but have to do to keep food on the table, but if he was going to be

playing at threading beads in crèche anyways, it's no harm to be making a few quid off it,' said one parent we spoke to, whose two-year-old son makes up to 30 necklaces a day, easing his crèche fee by 50 per cent.

'And our older girl loves colouring in, so she doesn't really mind that instead of colouring in a picture of a rocket ship, she's colouring in the bumper of a Renault Clio with a spray gun. They still get breaks for yoghurt and naps and all that kind of thing, so it's probably not all that different to how crèche used to be, except we don't cry as much when our wages come in at the end of the month and then instantly disappear.'

The government is hoping the scheme will prove popular enough to dissuade the country from demanding a sensible system that makes going back to work worthwhile to parents, for which ministers have no plan whatsoever.

MOTORING

![Motorway scene with parking meters installed along the M50, under gantry signs reading "Gach Treo Eile ALL OTHER ROUTES M50", "R139", and "Calafort Átha Cliath DUBLIN PORT"]

PARKING METERS INSTALLED ALONG M50

Fullmindness

It might sound obvious, but get out into nature. Take off your shoes. Walk around naked for a while. Grow your hair. Build a hut. Simply ignore the local county council's pleas to vacate the roundabout. This is your time. You won't even hear those car horns after a while.

NEW parking meters with an extended maximum period of ten hours are to be installed along the M50, with the aim of generating €500 million in the first year of operation, WWN can confirm.

Motorists stationary for more than two minutes will be required to spend a minimum of €3 to avoid being clamped under the new measures.

Over 5,000 electronic meters will cater for 20 separate zones and will coincide with a brand new M50 app, which will allow motorists to simply text their current location on the motorway.

'On any given day, a motorist could be charged hundreds of euros for using the motorway'

However, motorists have slammed the new meters as a 'money racket', pointing out that tickets will only be valid in their designated area, forcing motorists to purchase several on their journey as they eventually pass from one zone to the next.

'On any given day, a motorist could be charged hundreds of euros for using the motorway,' said Sinn Féin spokesperson Cathal Ó Something.

In a reply, Minister for Transport Shane Ross defended the new meters, stating, 'It was either charge for parking or charge people for rent.'

The new meter contract was awarded to an Isle of Man company owned by businessman Denis O'Brien.

RECYCLING

LOCAL ALCOHOLIC INSTALLS BOTTLE BIN OUTSIDE HOME

SICK to death of loading the boot of his car with bags of bottles every few days, one Waterford man has taken recycling to a whole new level, installing his own dedicated bottle bin outside his home.

Self-confessed functioning alcoholic Martin Croke said the new brown bottle bin will take all the hassle and shame out of his life, now that he doesn't have to travel 10 kilometres every time he wants to 'dump the evidence'.

'I picked the brown bottle bin as I always drink the same German wheat beer,' Croke began, proudly emptying last night's deposits before revealing some recycling insider information. 'Not that separating the coloured bottles matters. The collection truck empties all the different coloured bottles into the same trailer anyway.

'There's nothing worse than the shame of driving up to a bottle bin with a car boot full of bottles to see some smug prick who knows you with a small box of four empty long-necks. At least now I can just recycle in peace without being judged by my peers.'

Mr Croke is the first person in Ireland to install his own dedicated bottle bin outside his home, raising calls for waste management providers to implement their own bottle wheelie bins.

'I'd fill up this baby every two weeks,' Croke explained, due to the sheer volume of his drinking. 'It's a lot of beer, but I'm saving a fortune on petrol.'

Despite owning his own bottle bin, the son-of-two still manages to leave empty boxes and plastic bags beside the skip.'

'Old habits die hard,' Croke concluded.

ENTIRE BANK BRANCH STOLEN OVERNIGHT

GARDAÍ in County Tipperary are appealing for eyewitnesses to come forward after an entire branch of Bank of Ireland was stolen by raiders overnight.

Staff at the Bank of Ireland branch in the town of Murt were left devastated this morning to find the 2,400-square-metre building gone when they arrived to work at 9 a.m., with nothing only the bank's foundations left at the scene, along with three stolen diggers and two cranes used in the robbery.

'There is literally nothing left of the three-storey building,' bank manager Kevin Federton told WWN. 'They even took the car park out the back.'

How the raiders removed the large bank building without waking local residents has yet to be explained. One man, who lives beside the bank, believes he heard a loud bang at around 4 a.m. this morning.

'I thought nothing of it until I got up to feed the dogs this morning and noticed the whole bank next door was gone,' Tommy Rotchford recalled. 'They were clever enough to erect supports so my house didn't fall down and wake me. They must have been pros.'

CCTV footage showed raiders loading the bank onto the back of three parallel truck trailers, which

Suburban Dictionary

'I will, yeah': I will not be doing the thing you just asked me to do.

slowly took off into the night with the building in tow, along with all its contents, including the safe, several ATMs, computers, a canteen, the upstairs offices, a car park, and even the wheelie bins.

Gardaí have asked people who come across anyone trying to sell the listed items above to contact Murt garda station. This is the fourth stolen bank building in the area in only a matter of months, leading detectives to believe it may be the same gang involved.

NATURE

STARLING MURMURATION SPELLS 'PISS OFF' FOR MESMERISED VISITORS

HUNDREDS of visitors have flocked to County Meath this month to witness a mesmerising murmuration of starlings creating unique shapes and messages in the evening sky, WWN can confirm.

Thousands of starlings gathered over the village of Nobber in the sky yesterday evening in their usual display. But revellers were greeted with a special message in the sky.

In a picture taken by amateur photographer Daniel Ryan, the words 'Piss Off' can be clearly seen crafted out by the swirling birds.

'There were hundreds of amazed people staring at the starlings, making weird noises of appreciation, when the birds suddenly started swooping closer to us,' Ryan recalled. 'They seemed quite aggressive and at one point I could have sworn the birds mimicked a hand giving the middle finger.

'By the time I got out my camera to take the snap, they had the words spelled out in the sky, which was perfect timing,' he added.

Other witnesses have also since come forward, stating that the birds spelled out other words, too, including the phrases 'Private Function' and 'Nosy Pricks'.

'I guess this particular breed of starling is more private than others. They just want to be left the fuck alone,' expert in starling behaviour Dr Terence Holden told WWN.

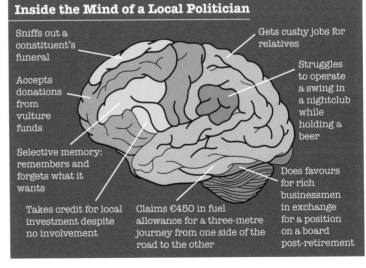

Inside the Mind of a Local Politician

Sniffs out a constituent's funeral

Accepts donations from vulture funds

Selective memory: remembers and forgets what it wants

Takes credit for local investment despite no involvement

Claims €450 in fuel allowance for a three-metre journey from one side of the road to the other

Gets cushy jobs for relatives

Struggles to operate a swing in a nightclub while holding a beer

Does favours for rich businessmen in exchange for a position on a board post-retirement

POLICING

MANHUNT FOR CRAZED KILLER CALLED OFF AFTER PHRASE 'MANHUNT' FOUND TO BE SEXIST

AN investigation into a brutal quadruple murder in Waterford has been placed on hold, as debate rages on about the correct terminology to use in today's more enlightened times, after confirmation that the phrase 'manhunt' is both outdated and insensitive.

Although Waterford remains in shock after the as-yet-unnamed victims of the frenzied attack were found earlier today in a house on the outskirts of the city, attempts to find and apprehend the perpetrator remain at a standstill, as gardaí await a team of language specialists, human-rights activists and woke bros to come back to them with a more gender-neutral

> **'Even though the killer may have been assigned as male at birth, they may identify as a woman now'**

term for a manhunt, which may take some time.

'To say that we're on a "manhunt" suggests that we are certain the culprit is a man, when in actual fact it could have been a woman,' said Garda Harry Jones, just scratching his hole waiting around at the crime scene.

'Also, even though the killer may have been assigned as male at birth, they may identify as a woman now. Therefore, it's insensitive for us to assume their gender based on their outward appearance. And remember, in instances of gender fluidity, the murderer may have identified as a man when the killing took place, but as a woman at all other times. No matter what way you look at it, we can't say we're on a "manhunt". Have you any idea how much shit we'd get on Twitter over it?'

If caught, the killer faces a mandatory life sentence.

[UPDATE]: If caught, the killer faces a mxndatory life sentence.

Community text alerts

Tom Tracey keeps looking at the special school's planning permission for its vital extension. Expect objection, the fucking bollocks.

FASHION

LOCAL MAN ROCKING SAME JACKET FOR 30 YEARS NOW

Community text alerts

Council is asking locals to stop testing if the 'Caution Wet Paint' sign outside Centra is for real. It is. We just checked.

'I've got bathroom towels older than you, kid,' opened up local man Dessie Casey, in defence of his fawn suede jacket, which he purchased from Woolworths in Waterford in 1989.

'This jacket is a part of me now. I've been wearing it so long that when I don't, people fail to recognise me on the street,' he added, caressing the sleeve against his face, almost romantically.

Despite attempts to recycle it in the numerous charity shops

> **'This jacket is a part of me now. I've been wearing it so long that when I don't, people fail to recognise me on the street'**

around Waterford, wife Tanya Casey said she has come to accept her husband's garment, which they have since christened with the name Betsy.

'Betsy was probably the reason I first laid eyes on Dessie in 1989,' Tanya recalled, reminiscing about the first time the couple met. 'Back then, she was a lot more vibrant and not frayed around the elbows. She's seen a lot of good and bad times, and I suppose Dessie and I have a sentimental attachment to her at this stage. He'll never part with her and I realise that now.'

Dad jackets can be worn for up to 35 years before they have to be decommissioned under a state law, which stipulates that no man, woman or child in Ireland can wear a jacket for more than 35 years, unless they work in civil-servant roles.

ww news

Waterford Whispers News

WORLD NEWS

AMERICA

AMERICANS BURN DOWN HOTEL EARMARKED FOR IRISH IMMIGRANTS

AMERICA'S infestation of illegal Irish immigrants, now estimated to be 50,000, cannot go on any longer, according to local Bostonians who last week took the unprecedented step of burning down a hotel that had been earmarked for immigrants.

'They keep to themselves, don't mix well, commit crimes, and don't accept the American way of life. Calling them

Fullmindness

Were you sad once? Now's the perfect time to wade into the conversations of those who have genuine mental-health issues, just to talk about yourself.

> **'Why can't their own country look after them? I don't see why we have to take them'**

migrants is fucking generous, too. They're welfare tourists,' confirmed one anti-Irish protester.

'Why can't their own country look after them? I don't see why we have to take them. It's not America's problem,' added another protester, who was concerned about the IRA presence now in America.

The burning down of the hotel, which Irish immigrants allegedly

stay in before choosing to illegally remain in America, is reminiscent of another recent incident in New York, which also resulted in a hotel burning down, seemingly a statement of how resented Irish people's presence is in America.

The understandable animosity toward a corrupt and work-shy group of filthy immigrants, who even avail of public services paid for by the taxpayer, has, however, been met with surprise back in Ireland.

'Jesus, we'd never treat people this harshly. And all the lies they're spreading about the Irish over there. It's disgusting. I just can't imagine anything like that happening here,' confirmed one Irish person.

THE MIDDLE EAST

ISRAEL FINALLY RECOGNISES PALESTINE FOLLOWING LOCAL MAN'S RELENTLESS TWEETS

THE United Nations, along with NATO and dozens of world leaders, have today congratulated 58-year-old Michael O'Riordan for singlehandedly pressuring Benjamin Netanyahu to finally recognise Palestine as a sovereign state, putting an end to decades of land-grabbing and conflict.

Following nine years of relentless tweets, Facebook posts, and lengthy debates in internet comment sections and anti-Israeli forums, the Waterford man was hailed a hero the world over for his persistent sharing of Israeli crimes, which in turn forced Israel's leader to make a complete U-turn on Palestine.

'From today, Israel and its partners across the world will now officially recognise the Palestinian state and begin the process of handing back any settlements we have taken over the past 60 years,' Mr Netanyahu stated at a televised press conference today to announce the shocking truce.

'After seeing thousands of social-media posts about our heinous and horrible crimes committed against the Palestinian people, I have no other option but to admit this country's wrongdoings over the years, and I would like to thank Irishman Michael O'Riordan for pointing it out to us.'

In an emotional speech, Benjamin Netanyahu held up several of Michael's graphic Facebook posts, some of which depicted dead children who were allegedly killed by the Israeli regime.

'Until accidentally seeing Michael's posts while looking through some Mossad files, I had no idea of the devastation and hurt we had caused,' Netanyahu added, now sobbing uncontrollably. 'Thankfully we've been shown the error of our ways and we can start building a brighter future together for our two beautiful states, and live in peace and harmony for the remainder of our co-existence.'

Speaking from his flat in Waterford city earlier, Michael O'Riordan welcomed the news, stating that he always knew that someday his online posting would pay off

'Fucking knew it would work,' O'Riordan insisted. 'You can only get away with that shite for so long before everyone starts saying "Hey, that's cat, boy!", ya know what I mean?'

The part-time taxi driver said he will now focus his attention on other illegal occupations around the world in a bid to sort them out.

'Give me another few years at this craic and we'll have world peace,' O'Riordan promised, now looking up Afghanistan's Wikipedia page.

WWN Was There

𝔚aterford 𝔚hispers News

President John F Kennedy visits Ireland, 26 June 1963

What we said then: A joyous day for Ireland. The Irish American Catholic president was much like any ordinary man – no different from you or I – only he was easily eight-foot tall and his voice carried across several counties without the aid of a voice-projection device. His skin shone with the force of a thousand suns. He cured the lame and sick simply by looking at them. A farmer, in his 60s, broke through the crowd, wept and begged the president to adopt him and be his father. The president cradled him in his arms for an hour.

What we say now: Reporters sometimes get swept up in the moment and play loose with the truth. As we all know, President Kennedy was at least nine-feet tall and impregnated all Irish women he encountered on his visit.

GUN LAWS

AMERICA TO BAN SINGLE-USE BULLETS

THE United States of America has voted overwhelmingly to support a countrywide ban on all single-use bullets, such as the lead round-nose, semi-jacketed and full metal jacket bullets, WWN can confirm.

The ban could be enshrined in US law by as early as July 2019 in a bid to cut down on the number of bullets entering the food chain. It is believed that bullets now account for 96 per cent of America's total waste.

The news comes as researchers found dangerous metals, such as lead, appearing in various foods such as salt, bread and even tap water in some parts of the country.

'Texas is currently the most contaminated state when it comes to single-use bullets,' said a report

published in *The Washington Post*. Bullet fragments have been detected in 38 per cent of human waste in Texas. They are highly toxic and can cause diseases such as cancer and a newly discovered ailment called 'bullet hole'.

The first instance of 'bullet hole' was diagnosed in 2012, during a routine examination of a Texas man complaining of terrible cramps in his stomach, before he was admitted to a Dallas hospital.

'Bullet hole is caused by ingesting too many tiny pieces of bullet which then perforate the lining of the stomach and intestines, causing severe inflammation,' says Dr Todd Chamberson, who first treated the patient seven years ago. 'Since then

we're seeing more and more cases and it's all down to the use of single-use bullets.'

From July, all single-use bullets could be replaced with recyclable designs, which can be used again and again.

'Extracting bullets from people and animals for reuse isn't ideal, but it's a start in helping our environment,' the doctor concluded.

IT'S no surprise to those who know Michael O'Leary that the Ryanair man has triumphed yet again in a bid to reduce costs, maximise revenue and ensure customers get the cheapest flights imaginable.

Ryanair has once more turned to innovative practices within the aviation industry to ensure they remain top of the pile, this time axing one wing from every plane in its fleet, which could save the airline as much as €1 billion over the next few years.

A flicker of O'Leary's business genius re-emerged from the shadows

RYANAIR TO REMOVE ONE WING FROM EACH PLANE IN COST-CUTTING EXERCISE

today, after months of battling with unions and plotting a way to poison all union leaders without getting caught.

'The sawing began at about 7 a.m. this morning,' confirmed one contractor tasked with hacking the wings off existing Ryanair planes. 'One less wing is one less thing to have to

maintain, repair and constantly check up on.'

All excess wings will be sold on to airlines in south-east Asia, and all new Ryanair planes ordered will come with explicit instructions to stop at just the one wing.

'Customers will always complain. You can't please every moany bastard,' O'Leary said, responding to criticism of the cost-cutting exercise.

'Can they fly? Look, we'll just have to give it a crack and regardless of whether or not it works, we'll be playing that annoying arrived-on-time music.'

Health and fitness tip

Unused kettle bells make for great doorstops and paperweights.

YEMEN

AS Saudi Arabia continues to escalate its military activity in Yemen, committing war crime after war crime, many people have been left devastated at what this means for the innocent civilians caught up in the carnage meted out by UK- and US-manufactured weapons.

WWN has collected questions that thousands of people have been asking, as they contemplate the reality of the continued and senseless loss of life, which eerily echoes the inhumanity of previous conflicts and others still ongoing elsewhere.

With casual conversations at work, as well as conversations with friends, at social functions and in almost every other social interaction, no matter where it is, dominated completely by news of Yemen and the million at risk of famine, we endeavour to bring you the answers you want.

Suburban Dictionary

'He/she's a right gallery altogether': A person who resembles a postmodern art gallery.

'ANYTHING GOOD ON NETFLIX?' YOUR YEMEN WAR QUESTIONS ANSWERED

'Is *Wild Wild Country* on Netflix worth watching?'
Oh my God, it's so fucking good. Like, you'll ask yourself how you'd never heard of this crazy shit before. They're mental, like full-on cult mental.

'That *Annihilation* movie has Natalie Portman in it. She's class, but I'm not big on sci-fi. Is it worth the risk?'
While only slightly less riskier than the risk Yemen civilians take each day by simply existing, watching *Annihilation* if you're not a big sci-fi fan might not pay off, despite the fact the movie is a fantastic addition to that particular genre. The cinematography is amazing and, can we just say, it's great to see a movie fronted by an almost all-female cast. We're making progress, however slow it is, but we're making progress.

'*Breaking Bad*? Really, like, is it that fucking good? People do my head in recommending it.'
We feel you, honestly, but just think of all the conversations you can have with people once you've become passionate about the defining TV series of our time. Every conversation that should be punctuated with things like 'Yup, we'll just stand by idly and let death descend on Yemen' can instead become really rewarding dissections of where exactly Walter White started to become truly evil.

'Any decent, lighthearted stuff?'
We hear your concerns loud and clear. *Lovesick*; *American Vandal*; *To All the Boys I've Loved Before*; *Game Over, Man!*, and a variety of stand-up specials are what you're looking for, buddy. *Lovesick* is a hidden gem on Netflix. Can't recommend it enough, honestly.

NATURE

NEW biological research into the behaviour of plants has found strange electronic signals emitted from trees in the grips of suffocation by *Hedera* – commonly called ivy – indicating that trees actually quite like being choked to death.

Using sophisticated electronic probes, which read the various chemical and electrical reactions of plants, researchers at WIT in Waterford found 'climactic-like orgasms' emanating from mature trees being strangled by ivy.

'"Yeah, baby. Harder, just around the branch there. Yeah, that's it. Harder! All over my bark, you dirty little ivy slut," is basically a direct translation from the trees we've tested so far,' Professor Kevin Rogers told WWN, having spent years translating his findings into understandable phrases for humans.

'The Dutch elms are the worst. I can't even repeat what those filthy feckers say while being choked out by ivy. Trees aren't as innocent as you'd think,' he added.

In some instances, large amounts of sap was recorded seeping from some trees that were being choked, leading researchers to believe that most trees actually ejaculate when aroused enough.

'They love being choked,' Professor Rogers explained, while pointing to a graph depicting large spikes where the ivy was at its tightest. 'Kinky fuckers. I think they just love being dominated. Gaspers, we call them – constantly gasping for it.'

The groundbreaking new research is set to revolutionise how humans perceive plants and trees, with research indicating that 'death by erotic asphyxiation' is now the number-one goal of a tree.

TREES GET AROUSED WHEN IVY CHOKES THEM, NEW RESEARCH FINDS

Suburban Dictionary

'You were an accident, but we're glad we had you': The youngest child in every Irish family.

RELIGION

'I KEEP LEAVING DOORS OPEN': JESUS TALKS ABOUT BEING BORN IN A BARN

FOLLOWING a 2,000-year hiatus, Jesus Henry Christ talks to WWN about life, his latest book, and a range of bad habits he's picked up over the years, which he claims are direct consequences of being born in a barn.

We caught up with the only son of God in a city-centre Starbucks, where he was busy writing his latest gospel on an Apple iMac, dressed in the guise of the many fashion-conscious hipsters scattered around him.

'Is that a skinny mocha frappuccino now?' he replied to a call from a female staff member shouting the name 'Jesus of Nazareth', before turning to this reporter to apologise. 'Sorry, I'll be with you in a minute. These baristas always fuck up my order.'

Sitting back down with his upper lip caked in frothy skimmed milk, Jesus got straight into it. 'Thanks for agreeing with my agent to meet me here. It's hard to find places where I just blend into the background. My fans can be a little extreme.'

'No, thank *you*,' I replied, intrigued by his latest book. 'Your agent says you're going back to your roots with this one?'

> **'Mental health is so in right now. It's a no-brainer and we need a big newspaper and publisher on board to help sell it'**

'Yeah, Dad thinks the last one was a bit too controversial,' he said, referring to the millions of people who have died as a direct result of the Bible. 'Fair enough, we sold billions of them, but the fallout was insane. People being burned at the stake, crucifixions – it wasn't ideal.'

'So, what's the premise? Is it fiction again, or what?' I asked, apprehensively.

'It's my life story: *Born in a Barn*,' Jesus said. 'No more fairytales. No ghostwriters. Just a simple autobiography outlining my psychological issues growing up and how I overcame them.

'Mental health is so in right now. It's a no-brainer and we need a big newspaper and publisher on board to help sell it.'

'So, it's a book about your problems?' I ask, knowing the saturated market Jesus was attempting to jump into.

'Well, yeah. Stuff like how I'm for ever leaving doors open, that kind of thing,' Jesus said, now checking out a female member of staff as she passed.

'Hmm, but are the issues you have life-threatening or relatable to today's society? I don't see how leaving doors open can …'

'No, no, no, listen. If you leave a plane door open, what happens, huh? Or a car door. Fucking dangerous, that.'

'But Jesus, it feels a little empty, dare I say shallow? Considering all the massive problems people have these days with stress, anxiety, depression …'

'Ah yeah, just fucking typical. If Meghan Sparkle or whatever her name is farted wrong, you'd have a ten-page spread on it,' Jesus retorted, the wounds on his hands now starting to weep in anger.

'Being born in a barn doesn't really constitute a heart-wrenching book. It seems like you're only doing it for the sake of it, Jesus. Like, you don't actually care about your so-called condition, but just want to benefit from it?'

'Okay, okay. What about that post-traumatic stress thing, then? I was nailed on a fucking cross for three days, lad. We could play on something like that.'

'Yeah, Jesus. I just don't think the public will go for it, ya know? But do please keep trying. It has been 2,000 years since your last book, so take your time. No need to just rush a book out for the sake of it.'

'Obviously my problems aren't good enough for you people any more. I died for your sins and all I get is them thrown back in my face.'

'Now, now, Jesus, don't be like that. It's just a tough market out there …'

With that, Jesus slammed down his iMac in disgust and stood up, staring at this reporter for what appeared to be an eternity.

'I could actually kill you right now with my mind, but I won't,' he said, before leaving me with his Starbucks bill.

RELIGION

GOD IGNORES YET ANOTHER PRAYER NOTIFICATION ON HIS PHONE

TV guide

Vogue Williams Opening an Envelope: RTÉ2 continues its dominance of the coveted youth demographic with this smash-hit series beloved by the 35s and over. Hot television property Virgin Media will be kicking themselves they couldn't wrestle Vogue away from RTÉ2. Vogue will turn up to the opening of an envelope and seven to ten RTÉ cameras will be there to capture it.

Tuesday, 10 p.m., RTÉ2.

GLANCING at the home-screen preview of the latest prayer notification on his iPhone XS, God the Almighty made a mental note to look up how to turn off the 'blasted notifications' once and for all, which are now running into the tens of billions.

'Dear God, please take care of my grandad as he is very ...' pinged yet another preview, as the five-billion-year-old began planning the final stages of Earth's total annihilation.

'Right, fuck this. I can't be arsed looking up how to switch this off,' he muttered. 'Now, where did I put those doomsday comets?

> **'Hopefully this will cause a huge flood and they'll all be ... No, no, wait. I promised them I wouldn't!'**

'Ah balls, I used them on those ridiculous dinosaurs. What on earth was I thinking with those things?'

'Praise Allah, please, can you bring world peace to the ...' pinged another.

Now desperately looking for anything to make the humans stop pestering him, God picked up his trusty magnet and began shifting the poles.

'Hopefully this will cause a huge flood and they'll all be ... No, no, wait. I promised them I wouldn't!' he said, remembering his rainbow promise, before deciding just to open the prayer app's settings to see if he could figure out how to turn off the notifications himself.

'Oh! That was actually quite easy. We'll keep you little shits for another day,' he then concluded.

SAUDI ARABIA

'AT LEAST THEY'RE NOT ANGRY ABOUT THAT FAMINE WE CAUSED'

AS they continue to bumble their way through explaining to an outraged international community how they accidentally premeditated the torture and execution of journalist Jamal Khashoggi, King Salman and Prince Mohammed bin Salman have been relieved to discover that world leaders are less vexed about the bloodshed and famine they're carrying out in Yemen.

Bombing key sources of agricultural cultivation in Yemen, the Saudi royal family are orchestrating a soon-to-be irreversibly catastrophic famine in war-torn Yemen, likely resulting in the death of millions. Crown Prince Mohammed bin Salman, however, is counting his lucky stars that the heat remains on the callous and evil murder of Khashoggi in Saudi Arabia's embassy in Turkey.

'Imagine how annoyed and outraged everyone would be if they got word of all those war crimes in Yemen. Jeez, we would be

in serious trouble then,' said Prince bin Salman on the routine bombing of Yemen, aided by the multi-billion-dollar purchase of US and UK arms.

While the Saudis are unhappy at the scrutiny they've been placed under as a result of Khashoggi's murder, their spirits remain high, thanks to nobody taking them to task on the now two-year-long famine.

'The threat of sanctions, expelling of diplomats, all for one journalist? Shit, imagine what trouble we'd be in for systematically orchestrating the starvation of a whole country. The consequences, which we definitely aren't going to suffer, don't bear thinking about,' added bin Salman as he took in the crowds at the Future Investment Initiative summit in Riyadh.

While some high-profile CEOs pulled out of the summit after Khashoggi's murder, they are expected to make a swift return with their chequebooks once the media's glare fades away.

GLOBAL WARMING

CLIMATE CHANGE WARNING AS VANILLA ICE NOW 80 PER CENT SMALLER

IN perhaps the starkest warning to the human race about the ravaging effects of climate change on our world, early-90s rapper Vanilla Ice is now 80 per cent smaller than he was at the height of his popularity, based on new aerial images of the musician.

Coming in at 1.8 metres during his 'Ice Ice Baby' heyday, Vanilla Ice was recently measured at just 14 inches, after decades of man-made damage to the Earth's natural defence against harmful sun rays, which has resulted in irreversible changes to our climate and the devastation of all ice-based stuff in the would.

Real name Vernertla Von Icetenstein, the singer-turned-man is in genuine danger of disappearing altogether, with the world's politicians either

> **'At first when he showed up 6 inches shorter, we all just thought he'd gotten rid of that stupid fucking stand-up hair'**

ignorant of the impending disaster or simply opting to do nothing about it.

'We are putting the government under pressure to do something about climate change, or one day our children won't even have a Vanilla Ice. We'll just have to tell them stories about it,' said a climate-change awareness group.

'The shrinking of Vanilla Ice has been ignored for too long. Okay, at first when he showed up 6 inches shorter, we all just thought he'd gotten rid of that stupid fucking stand-up hair. But then, no, he was a foot shorter one year. He was half his height the next. He doesn't even fit his Polar Vanilla Ice cap anymore. This is unprecedented human shrinkage, causing untold damage to the wildlife that depend on him for survival.'

Alarmingly, the group have also warned that after Vanilla Ice, Ice-T might be next, followed by Ice Cube.

'You can say you don't care about Vanilla, but this is going to keep happening, until it happens to an ice-based popstar you do care about,' they sobbed.

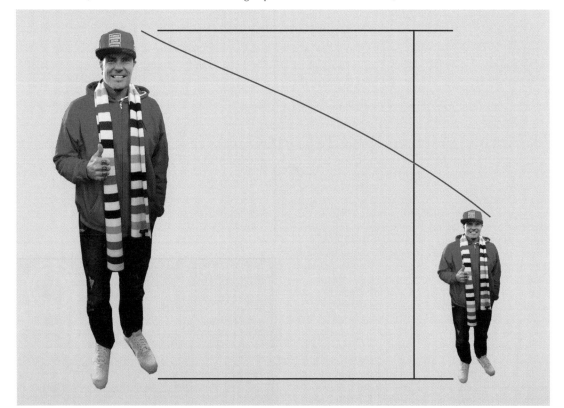

EXCLUSIVE

THE WORLD'S OLDEST PEOPLE KEEP DYING AND NO ONE KNOWS WHY

WITH the official oldest person in the world announced this week as 116-year-old Japanese woman Kane Tanaka, WWN investigated one of the most cursed Guinness records to date, which has so far taken every single person who has held the prestigious title.

Investigating the records of all the oldest people in the world, we started with the very oldest, Jeanne Calment, a 122-year-old French woman who died suddenly in 1997.

'Just like nearly all of her predecessors, Calment was just your stereotypical supercentenarian, enjoying life to the fullest,' said historian Dr James Patterson. 'Then, on 4 August that year, she suddenly just drops dead, despite never being sick before a day in her life.'

Taking up the reins that same year, 115-year-old Maggie Barnes then became Guinness's new poster girl, but her new role was also short-lived, when she just died from apparently nothing.

'Only one year after Ms Calment died, Barnes soon followed,' Dr Patterson added. 'In fact, anyone who has held the title of world's oldest person only lasted a year at most, with some not even lasting that long, which is really odd and very suspicious. What on earth is happening to these poor people?'

Experts have speculated that the stress of holding such a title could be the main cause of their sudden, untimely deaths.

'It's a lot to take on, so I'm sure it's very stressful at the top,' one expert insisted.

Other possibilities include a serial killer who may be preying on the world's oldest people, and who remains, for the moment, at large.

More on this story as it develops.

SAUDI ARABIA

'I'VE HAD THOUSANDS OF PEOPLE MURDERED – WHAT'S YOUR POINT?'

'Woah! Wait. Hold on a second here, guys. You're suddenly pissed that I killed one measly journalist? Seriously?' Crown Prince of Saudi Arabia Mohammed bin Salman addressed the world's press last night in an eye-opening speech, calling out the CIA and other critics who have accused him of crossing a 'red line'.

'Fucking red line? I'll give you a red line. We're literally starving ten million people in Yemen and you're getting on our case over having some bad-mouthed hack hacked to death. Please, even my moral compass points to hypocrisy here,' bin Salman continued.

'We're using the weapons you sold us to annihilate innocent civilians, for Allah's sake. You're even refuelling our planes mid-air during the bombing campaigns. You're buying our oil. You watch us decapitate hundreds of people every year, some of whom are

women who were raped because they tried to retaliate, and only now you're suddenly concerned?'

'Seriously, have a logical think about it there to yourselves,' the prince stated, staring down at the gathered reporters.

His comments come as pressure mounts on the Saudi royal over a recent report by US intelligence agencies that claims he ordered the murder of journalist Jamal Khashoggi, who was lured to the Saudi consulate in Istanbul on 2 October, before being killed and reportedly dismembered.

'Well, it was hardly the fucking Tooth Fairy that chopped him up to

make a buck on his teeth, was it?' Bin Salman retorted. 'Seriously, if I go down for this, it will be a total embarrassment to the family. Do me for something juicy and worthwhile, like genocide, or try me as a war criminal, but not for chopping up some loser in an embassy – I order hits like that in my sleep.'

Fullmindness

Remember, when meditating, don't think about how everyone on this planet is born alone and will eventually die alone. That's a big no-no.

'I'M STILL IN DEBT': WE INTERVIEW IRELAND ON ITS 70TH BIRTHDAY

ON 17 April this year, the Republic of Ireland turned 70 years old, in what was to be a joyous and momentous occasion for the sovereign nation. However, these celebrations were marred by the fact that the ageing country was being run into the ground by its current rulers, leaving it no other option but to speak out to this fine publication.

'They sold all my woods to the mainland,' Ireland began, wiping microbeads of plastic from its mouth, known locally as the Shannon estuary. 'The bastards are even selling my fish, too. Can you believe that?'

Reaching for its pint of Guinness, the now frail and psychologically damaged island went on.

'You know they threw a load of babies in graves, so they did. Didn't even bother to leave a mark on me as to where they are,' it added, now turning its attention to the banks.

'There's this crowd going around lending people money for small pieces of me, promising the eejits that they'll actually own the lots. Then, when they can't afford to pay it back, they swoop in and take the pieces for themselves. It's gas when you think about it. I'm billions of years old. No one owns me. I fucking own youse, ya thicks!'

Complaining of aches in its landfill sites and a poisoned bloodstream pumped full of raw sewage, Ireland said it wasn't too optimistic about its future health.

'Most of my arteries are clogged full of rubbish. They're even cutting down the trees in towns and cities now, too. This so-called management company they call the government are doing sweet F all for me, despite the main man being a doctor,' Ireland spluttered.

Now tired from its rant, Ireland sat back in its seabed before concluding, 'I've a bad case of humans. I'll be lucky to see 90 at this rate.'

> **Health and fitness tip** +
>
> It's important to exercise your lateral muscles, whatever the fuck they are.

PC WORLD BRANCH BURNED TO THE GROUND BY ALT-RIGHT MOB

FIREFIGHTERS spent this morning battling a blaze at a branch of PC World in Workington in the UK after an angry mob, believed to be affiliated with several extremist far-right groups, set it ablaze.

Traveling on buses from nearby Cockermouth on the A66, hordes of far-right protesters (mostly men) could be heard shouting 'You can't say anything these days' and seemed to be demanding an end to the politically correct culture they erroneously believed PC World to be responsible for starting and fostering.

'Can't say nowt about no one, not even coloureds,' raged one man who had 'had enough' of being repeatedly arrested and sent to jail for racially motivated attacks.

'And don't get me started on the birds, they do my nut in,' shared a serial sex offender who was breaking his bail conditions to be at the arson attack.

Brave and courageous branch manager Martin Melvin sought to talk to the mob in a bid to calm them down before they entered the store. He spoke with WWN earlier today, despite being visibly shaken.

'I tried to tell them the mistake they'd made. We just sell computers, shit like that. But then once they spotted that we're actually called Currys PC World these days … Well, as you can imagine, they fucking lost their minds,' Mr Melvin shared.

CHINA

IRISH-BUILT SECTION OF GREAT WALL OF CHINA SUFFERING FROM PYRITE

THE Chinese government is looking into ways to recoup the money it paid to a group of unscrupulous Irish property developers who built a section of the Great Wall of China, which is now badly affected by pyrite damage, WWN can confirm.

Built by Hanratty, Morgan & O'Farrell, a firm which has entered and exited NAMA on 37 separate occasions, the offending section was first constructed in the mid-15th century by the company, but the Chinese government is said to have been left irate at the large cracks appearing, thanks to the use of pyrite.

'The rest of the wall looks fine. I mean, repairs here and there, but this one section is crumbling into nothing and is structurally unsound. We demand to be compensated for the poor job,' one spokesman for the Chinese government said.

Despite attempting to contact the offices of Hanratty, Morgan & O'Farrell multiple times, Chinese officials have been unable to get answers from the firm.

Speaking to WWN, a spokesperson from HMO explained that they bore no responsibility for the devastating building defects.

'Look, if something needs fixing, we'll happily do it. We'll send on our rates. Our lads don't do this

Health and fitness tip

Talking about going to the gym is better for your core than actually going to the gym.

> **'That's a slur to the good name of our lads. So look, just so there's no hard feelings, we'll accept a top-up fee for our guys'**

sort of stuff for peanuts, though, so get the chequebook out,' the HMO official explained, before denying the presence of pyrite in any materials they used to build the Chinese wall.

'That's a slur to the good name of our lads. So look, just so there's no hard feelings, we'll accept a top-up fee for our guys.'

IKEA

IKEA CELEBRATES ONE MILLIONTH RUINED RELATIONSHIP

'Whatever we've won, she'll waste it on some stupid shit that I'll have to spend a weekend putting together'

THE Dublin branch of Swedish furniture and lifestyle store IKEA has celebrated its one millionth blazing row between a couple trying to pick out what would look best in their house, WWN can reveal.

Michael Williams and his girlfriend Charlene Harris had a five-alarm meltdown in the Bathroom Solutions aisle over why they needed to buy a new shower caddy for holding soaps and gels, if Williams was just going to 'throw everything on the ground'.

The ferocious row became the one millionth kick-off in the Dublin store since it opened in July 2009, and Williams and Harris continued to snipe at each other, despite the explosion of confetti cannons and balloons cascading around them, as

'Celebration' by Kool & the Gang blared over the speaker system.

'Whatever we've won, she'll waste it on some stupid shit that I'll have to spend a weekend putting together,' moaned Michael Williams, storming outside for a smoke.

'Half the stuff he puts together falls apart anyway, and he can fuck off if he thinks he's getting a bag of Daims after this,' hissed Charlene Harris, sitting on a display sofa having a good old fume.

Meanwhile, a spokesperson for IKEA has stated the company is very open to arguments between same-sex couples, married couples, couples in polyamorous relationships, and people arguing with themselves.

Community text alerts

Fifth annual Pierce Brosnan Drove Through Tramore Once Festival to take place this weekend.

RELIGION

MIX-UP SEES THOUSANDS OF PAEDOPHILES ARRIVE AT VATICAN FOR SEX ABUSE CONFERENCE

APOLOGISING profusely for the mix up, the Catholic Church was forced to turn away thousands of sheepish paedophiles from the entrance of the Vatican after they arrived to attend a Vatican sex abuse conference.

'In hindsight, we see why they bought tickets,' Vatican spokesperson Father Gio Padre said, gently chuckling. 'If I were a paedophile

'In hindsight, we see why they bought tickets'

and I heard the Vatican was hosting a "sex abuse conference" and had invited 190 leaders of religious orders,

I can see why they'd think this was an opportunity to learn, to get a few pointers and the like.'

In fact, the conference was convened by Pope Francis in a bid to provide the Vatican with its bi-weekly good PR when it comes to safeguarding children and learning from past mistakes which were made on purpose.

The conference represents just the 408th time the Catholic Church has gathered to promise to 'get tough' on abuse, before once again slinking away to the shadows to carry on as normal.

'I flew all the way here from the seminary,' one irate paedophile told WWN. 'Now I'm being turned away and told there'll be no PowerPoint presentation on how to be moved to another parish. I want a refund.'

Topics for discussion at the conference included how to talk to victims, and how to pledge tough, zero-tolerance measures against abuse and then do the opposite.

SCIENCE

NEUROLOGISTS DISCOVER PART OF BRAIN THAT TELLS YOU TO GO DRINKING WHEN YOU'VE €29 TO YOUR NAME

SOME of the world's leading brain scientists believe that they may have isolated a group of synapses deep within the human brain that cause otherwise rational people to hit the pub on a weekday, even though they've got fuck-all funds and a load of bills due.

The neural area provisionally known as the 'Fuck-it cluster' appears to be more common in Irish people aged 18–90, with both men and women susceptible to rash decisions involving pints with the gang, paid for with credit cards and not worried about until the following month's billing date.

Neurologists have mooted a possible surgical procedure that would greatly extend the sobriety and bill-paying capabilities of those who possess an overactive 'Fuck-it cluster', but so far nobody has volunteered to undergo the surgery.

'It would seem that, for some, having nothing in the house except Koka noodles, with your broadband about to be cut off, isn't that much of a concern, especially when there's the possibility of a few pints,' mused a baffled Dr Darren Mallon, one of the leading brain people in the world.

'One would have thought that this self-destructive behaviour is something people would want to erase from their lives, but no, they're happy enough to be the type of person who can't resist a drinking session even when they still have 13 days to go until payday. So, eh, sure. Have at it, I suppose.'

In other news, Dr Mallon also stated that his team was very close to locating the synapse that tells you to call your ex for the ride at 3 a.m. when you've a skinful of drink in you.

> '**It would seem that, for some, having nothing in the house except Koka noodles, with your broadband about to be cut off, isn't that much of a concern**'

Animal facts

The whiskered bat is rarely sighted during daylight in Ireland, similar to third-level students.

WIKILEAKS

JULIAN ASSANGE CHARGED WITH SHOWING UP AMERICA FOR WHAT IT REALLY IS

WIKILEAKS founder Julian Assange has been arrested by police in London this morning and charged with showing up America for what it really is, WWN can confirm.

To be 100 per cent sure, UK police then arrested the 48-year-old

Community text alerts

A reminder that Áine Cleary's funeral tomorrow is strictly BYOF (Bring Your Own Fireworks).

for a second time on behalf of US authorities, just in case they didn't arrest him right the first time, and thus avoiding any crafty legalities the whistle-blower might have up his anti-establishment sleeve.

'What a joyous day this is for fans of illegal arrests aimed at suppressing news, journalism and the freedom of the press,' confirmed one media expert, who was taking his journalism certificates off the wall to burn them.

'According to the law, he should have been a free man by 2017, but you can't go showing up America

like that – exposing what a corrupt nation it really is and how its military regularly breaks international laws on human rights, while invading countries by using concocted intelligence for its own financial and territorial gain.

'America is the law and can do whatever it wants and Julian was stupid enough to expose that fact in a bad light, while us normal, obedient journalists just do what we're told.'

Assange was forcibly carried out of the Ecuadorian embassy after his asylum was suddenly and illegally revoked by the South American country, which has in no way benefited from its sudden U-turn.

'What America wants, America gets,' defended the Ecuadorian ambassador, now holding large brown envelopes with dollar signs on them. 'I can't say I'll miss him. He was starting to reek pretty badly.'

Elsewhere, US and UK authorities have apologised profusely for triggering an outbreak of 'Wake up, sheeple' social media statuses across the world.

TRUMP

'JUST GIVE US THE FUCKING OIL': TRUMP CALLS FOR CALM IN VENEZUELA

US President Donald Trump has called on the people of Venezuela to calm down following spiralling tensions in the South American country.

Addressing acting Venezuelan president Nicolás Maduro over his decision to close the country's embassy and consulates in the United States, Mr Trump appealed for reason, stating, 'Just give us the fucking oil and gold reserves, or we'll Gaddafi your fucking ass.'

The measured approach comes after opposition leader Juan Guaidó attempted to overthrow Maduro, offering him amnesty if he gave up his position and allowed the US-backed politician to replace him.

'You produce more oil than Saudi Arabia and yet your country is broke,' Trump pleaded, who admitted to being kept awake at night worrying about the fate of the Venezuelan people. 'Stop giving all your oil and gold away to Russia and China and let the US handle it for you so we can make everyone on the top end of Venezuelan society rich, including you,' before asking, 'Is that too much to ask?'

Mass protests calling for President Nicolás Maduro's removal has so far left 26 people dead and many more injured, with no end in sight of America's, Russia's or China's ongoing interests in yet another impoverished country they have no other reason to deal with, except to pillage for natural resources.

Animal facts

To scare away other birds, seagulls can mimic the cry of Dublin inner-city street traders.

RUSSIA STEALING MAGNETIC NORTH, REPORT CLAIMS

A damning new report published by the Canadian Security Intelligence Service has claimed that Russia has been slowly stealing magnetic north for the past 20 years, WWN can confirm.

The 467-page report stated that, from as early as 1999, Vladimir Putin secretly conspired with dozens of Russian billionaires to shift Earth's north magnetic pole. It is believed he oversaw the development of enormous underground magnetic facilities in Siberia, which have since slowly attracted and stolen the planet's liquid-iron outer core, known as the core field.

The worrying report estimated that magnetic north will be positioned in Russia's northern territory by the year 2035.

'We do not know why Russia is stealing magnetic north from the Canadian Arctic,' a spokesman for the intelligence service stated. 'Whatever the reason, it could be disastrous for the whole of humanity and have serious consequences for our current environment.'

Experts speculate that Russia may be taking the magnetic pole hostage in a power play against the West.

'Our fear now is that Russia may intend to start charging the rest of the world for using navigation systems which rely on magnetic north, which would also give them the upper hand in any future conflicts,' concluded a military expert.

EXCLUSIVE

SHOCKING FIVE OUT OF EVERY FIVE IRISH PEOPLE LIVING ABROAD ARE MIGRANTS

A shocking new survey on Irish citizens living abroad has found that a staggering five out of every five of them are classed as 'migrants', sparking confusion among the anti-migrant community here at home.

Furthermore, the survey also found that the overwhelming majority of Irish migrants living abroad were Caucasian and, much like foreign migrants living in Ireland, had similar reasons for moving from their homeland, usually in search of a better future.

'How could Irish abroad be migrants when they're not even black- or brown-skinned?' posed flustered anti-migration Facebook-page owner Mark O'Riordan. 'They're Irish people, with white skin and freckles, living in another country. How in God's name can they be labelled migrants?'

Referring to the *Collins English Dictionary* in defence of their findings, the team behind the survey defined a migrant as a 'person who moves from

> **'How could Irish abroad be migrants when they're not even black- or brown-skinned?'**

one place to another in order to find work or better living conditions', stating that this was the correct term to use, despite colour or racial prejudice.

'If that's the case, then the survey is stating that migrants coming over to Ireland are no different from the Irish living abroad, and that they should be treated and welcomed in the same way,' pointed out O'Riordan on his Facebook page.

'This is obviously a government-sponsored conspiracy, destined to desensitise Irish citizens into believing that every human being living on the island of Ireland has an equal and inalienable right to life, liberty and the pursuit of happiness, despite their race or religious beliefs – it's fucking madness and just typical hoodwinking by Fine Gael.'

BREAKING NEWS

A plane entered into a drastic course correction, back towards Dublin Aiport, just minutes after taking off from a runway earlier today, sparking panic among passengers, due to the fact that the pilot had left his phone charger behind, WWN can reveal.

The 2.45 p.m. flight to New York was forced into a sudden turnaround, shortly after a pilot could be heard loudly shouting from the cockpit 'Ah for fuck sake', prompting air traffic control officials to desperately get in touch with the aircraft.

The pilot's phone battery was believed to be just shy of 50 per cent charged. However, with much of the transatlantic flight spent on autopilot, the pilot felt he couldn't risk not being able to watch YouTube videos, peruse the Internet for memes, and

PLANE FORCED TO TURN BACK TO AIRPORT AFTER PILOT FORGETS PHONE CHARGER

anonymously post abuse and insults in plane-spotting forums.

In official exchanges reproduced by WWN below, the pilot and his co-pilot can be heard communicating with Dublin Airport authorities.

Pilot: 'Relax feckin' shouting at me, I'll be two minutes. I've just left me charger in the canteen. Seriously, stop shouting! Don't act like you've never forgotten something.'

Air traffic control: 'For Christ sake, Martin, this is the third time this week!'

Co-pilot: 'Is it an iPhone, Martin? Ya can borrow mine, like.'

Pilot: 'No, it's one of them feckin' weird Samsung ones, isn't it. Forget my fuckin' head if it wasn't screwed on.'

Co-pilot: 'I might buy a carton of fags then while you're nipping in for the charger.'

Pilot: 'Yeah, grand.'

Air traffic control: 'All right, lads. Just don't forget where you're parked this time. Don't want a repeat of Friday. Cleared for approach on Runway 10, you eejits.'

Passengers where then alerted as to why their scheduled flight required a U-turn via the onboard intercom, with many passengers going on to state their sympathy for the pilot.

'We've all been there, and yeah, we dropped 2,000 feet in about three seconds and did a loop-the-loop manoeuvre, and I vomited everywhere from the nausea, but c'mon, it could happen to anyone. I've lost my car keys more times than I care to mention,' asserted one passenger who didn't seem to mind the resulting 12-hour delay.

SAUDI ARABIA

THEY MURDER JOURNALISTS BUT LET WOMEN DRIVE – ARE THE SAUDIS REALLY THAT BAD?

IN this modern age, when we're so quick to become outraged in this politically correct world, Saudi Arabia, and its ruling Salman family, are getting a bit of flak for the alleged killing and dismembering of a journalist from *The Washington Post*.

But are the Saudis really that bad? After all, they recently allowed women the right to drive. WWN attempted to cut through all the noise to find a definitive answer.

None of us would like to be judged solely on our worst days, when we're a little tired, irritable or cranky. So should people really be allowed to criticise a regime that assassinates journalists when, you know, on their good days, sometimes they don't execute people for being homosexuals?

This snowflake culture we live in today doesn't seem to understand how the world works. And yes, okay, Saudi Arabia is using UK- and US-bought bombs to target Yemen's key agricultural resources, resulting in the onset of a deadly famine, but Saudi women are now allowed to have a choice in what they wear in public, so long as it's modest and they cover their hair.

Can any of us, if we're being honest, really stand up and say

we've never committed a litany of war crimes in Yemen? Let's not be hypocrites here, people.

The more we look into Saudi Arabia and the reforms of Prince Mohammed bin Salman, we can't help but see the good in the country. It's important not to judge a country on the one time they were actually caught assassinating an innocent journalist.

UPDATE 1: Sorry, we rushed to judgement. It turns out both US President Donald Trump and former President George Bush cosied up to King Salman over precious oil and trade. This is all kind of disgusting the more we think about it.

UPDATE 2: Sorry, false alarm. Turns out Barack Obama cosied up to King Salman, too, so he can't be that bad. We totally got caught up in that silly outrage business for a minute. It really is important to sit back, calm down and not have a super emotional reaction to watching a country get away with murdering journalists, and killing and starving kids in Yemen.

EXCLUSIVE

WOMEN DON'T FULLY UNDERSTAND MANSPLAINING, FINDS STUDY

RESULTS from a newly published study have revealed that a staggering number of women don't fully understand mansplaining and need it explained to them again because they are wrong about it.

'Mansplaining', mischaracterised as a man explaining something, often unsolicited, to a woman in a condescending manner, is not fully understood by as much as 92 per cent of the female population.

'Many of the women who partook in the study involuntarily were sat down by myself and my colleagues and told that an effort to explain something was not condescending but, in fact, a fair and reasonable attempt to insist they were just plain wrong,' explained head of the study, Professor Martin Yulin.

'You'd be amazed how many women didn't get it. Seriously, I tried to explain again a different way, how they were taking me up the wrong way, but would they listen?' added Yulin's frustrated colleague Greg Steinman.

'Ha! Tell me about it. Like talking to an attractive and beautiful brick wall …' added Paul Olsen, another team member behind the study.

The discovery that women don't understand the helpful interjections of

> ## 'Ha! Tell me about it. Like talking to an attractive and beautiful brick wall'

men with superior knowledge and understanding of any and all subjects, events and disciplines will trouble many people.

'God, that's shocking. I don't know if perhaps there's a way to help them grasp mansplaining and really nail down its meaning and intention. I'll make sure to take some extra time out of my day to properly explain it to the women in my life,' confirmed one man, Alan Mannigan, who spoke with WWN earlier today.

Suburban Dictionary

'The neck of you': A calm response to someone you have a disagreement with.

WWN Was There

𝖂𝖆𝖙𝖊𝖗𝖋𝖔𝖗𝖉 𝖂𝖍𝖎𝖘𝖕𝖊𝖗𝖘 News

Man lands on the Moon, 20 July 1969

What we said then: Yeah, nice try. 'Man' 'lands' on the 'Moon'. Pull the other one. We weren't born yesterday.

What we say now: I stand by the paper's statement.

Waterford Whispers News

RELIGION

VATICAN RAID SEES POPE AND THOUSANDS MORE ARRESTED IN IDEAL WORLD

AN early-morning raid on the Vatican by over 500 Interpol agents has seen the Pope and thousands of clergy members arrested as part of ongoing child abuse investigations spanning the past 50 years, WWN can confirm.

Treating the Vatican like any other multi-billion-euro company whose employees carried out decades of child abuse, agents stormed CEO Pope Francis's residence at 6 a.m. today in an ideal world, which is not too far from our own world, but a world just a little bit more intolerant to child sexual abuse than our own.

'If Google, Apple, or any other large multinational company had thousands of employees accused and charged for paedophilia offences, and proof that companies tried to cover this up, of course they'd be raided, and every document and file in their HQ would be searched,' explained ideal world lead Interpol investigator Detective Denis Kent.

Referring to the Vatican's own report that stated that one in every 50 Catholic priests have paedophilic tendencies, Kent explained, 'Just because the Vatican is based around a religion, it doesn't give it any more rights than any other company. They even pay the same rate of tax – nothing – so they should face the same laws.'

In the ideal world this morning, the Pope and his cardinals were detained in various holding cells across the region, will undergo intense interrogations, and are expected to be held for up to 72 hours, as part of the investigation into the biggest child-abuse cover-ups in modern ideal world history.

'We're going to see exactly what they know about the historic sexual abuse carried out by its staff,' Detective Kent added. 'We're going to search all their documents, all their

archives, absolutely everything we can find in their HQ. This was a long time coming, but inevitable all the same. Why wouldn't we raid the Vatican and its offices around the world? It would be criminal not to.'

Admitting to being a little late in their investigations, Kent also apologised to abuse victims the world over for the delay in finally investigating the Church.

'Even in an ideal world it's hard to convince senior people to investigate a religious order as big as the Vatican,'

Community text alerts

Bunch of chancers in suits going around Elm Park at the moment, knocking on doors and promising to solve the homeless crisis. Guards called.

he said. 'The main problem is a lot of people in power are afraid of the backlash, especially with the amount of information the Church has on them. You know the types.'

84

WW news

Waterford Whispers News

ENTERTAINMENT

EXCLUSIVE

JK ROWLING CONFIRMS HEDWIG SELF-IDENTIFIED AS A CAT

HARRY Potter author JK Rowling has yet again revealed a nugget of previously unknown information regarding a character from her wildly popular series of books, long after the series ended.

Hedwig, Harry Potter's pet owl, struggled with the fact that he self-identified as a cat, the author explained, despite there being no evidence whatsoever of such things throughout any of the series' seven books.

Much like the subject of Dumbledore's homosexuality, Hedwig's lifelong struggle of feeling like he actually belonged in the body of a cat was courageously fastened onto the character's backstory, long after the final book was published. It could well give a voice to owls that identify as cats, something long absent in fiction and young-adult fiction.

'It makes complete sense when you read the books back now. It's there plainly in print,' confirmed one superfan, pointing to passages which they had clearly changed with a biro, replacing the word 'owl' with 'cat'.

Heralded as a long-overdue step forward in animal rights, Hedwig's identity will be honoured going forward in any on-stage or on-screen iteration.

'Hedwig will either be played by a cat from now on, or by an owl that we can train to purr,' explained a source close to Rowling.

News surrounding Hedwig's identity is just the latest in a long line of authors making public new information about beloved characters. The tradition was first sparked by JRR Tolkien, who confirmed that Gollum was misunderstood and suffered from an eating disorder.

> 'Hedwig will either be played by a cat from now on, or by an owl that we can train to purr'

MOVIES

INDIANA JONES MOVIES BANNED FROM TV OVER CONCERNS THEY PROMOTE VIOLENCE AGAINST NAZIS

THE much-loved Indiana Jones movie series will be absent from TV screens this Christmas, after several far-right groups claimed that the whip-cracking archaeological adventures portrayed paint the Nazi party in an incredibly bad light, and may incite hatred and violence against the organisation.

Although the movies starring Harrison Ford have featured Dr Henry Walter 'Indiana' Jones battling communists, aliens, Chinese gangsters and undead cult leaders, Indy's most memorable foes have been the Nazis – Nazi soldiers, Nazi pilots, and Nazi sympathisers.

Throughout *Raiders of the Lost Ark* and *The Last Crusade*, the fedora-wearing protagonist has punched, whipped, diced with a propeller, and burned alive literally dozens of people loyal to Adolf Hitler, prompting

> **'What message is this sending to today's society? That it's perfectly fine to punch someone just because they believe they're part of a master race?'**

fascists all across the world to call for the movies to be banned.

'In this scene, we see a decent Nazi just doing his job, checking tickets on an airship, and what happens? A sucker-punch from Jones! Then he's thrown to what Indiana must surely hope is his death,' said John Smith, a member of Nazi rights group Rights for the Right.

'What message is this sending to today's society? That it's perfectly fine to punch someone just because they believe they're part of a master race, and that lower classes of human beings should be eradicated to ensure the dominance of the white race? You may say these are only movies, but it's an incredibly triggering time for Nazis like me. We shouldn't have to see our fellow fascists killed for your entertainment while we're kicking back after the big Christmas dinner.'

The move to ban Indiana Jones from TV has opened up debate about other Christmas favourites which show Nazis in a bad light. This could mean bans for *The Sound of Music* and *The Great Escape*, while Nazis are pushing for the 'tragic biopic' *Downfall* to take their place as a Christmas classic.

Suburban Dictionary

''Tis yourself': A greeting to demonstrate someone has correctly identified you as the person you yourself know yourself to be.

Waterford Whispers News

SHOWBIZ

AIDAN GILLEN PAYS VISIT TO NATIVE ENGLIRESCOTWALERICA

RENOWNED actor Aidan Gillen may be riding high on a wave of success following almost 20 years as one of the world's most sought-after character actors, but he has never forgotten his roots, as evidenced by his recent visit to his homeland of Englirescotwalerica.

Gillen was born in Englirescotwalerica in 1968, and although he left to pursue a career that took him from the London stage to the heights of Hollywood, he still hasn't lost his native accent from the small island off the coast of Ireland, Scotland, Wales, England, America, Sweden, bits of Australia, Canada and Mexico.

From Lord Petyr 'Littlefinger' Baelish in HBO's *Game of Thrones*, to John Reid in last year's Queen biopic *Bohemian Rhapsody*,

Gillen has made his trademark Englirescotwalerica drawl as iconic as Seán Connery's Scottish lilt and Arnold Schwarzenegger's Austrian brogue.

'Ahr shor, eesn't it garayte to be baahck in the ole home tahn agun,' mused Gillen, drinking a pint of Guhrnursh in his local pub.

'True that me and the lards would arlwars come to this purb to gert a feew pients whan I'm in tahn. It's just so march farn to be arble to cahm home everrah nar and then, whur everwan knows yar narm, but nobody annoys yar. Harleyward is garayte. It's whar I larve, but shar it'll narhvar bee hoooome. This, this is hoooome.'

Gillen's presence in town was very much enjoyed by his old friends, all of whom conversed in a tone that swung wildly from very loud to almost inaudible.

AZEALIA BANKS DEAD TO IRELAND AGED 27

AMERICAN rapper Azealia Banks was pronounced dead to Ireland today after a short battle with resentment and anger, WWN can confirm.

The 27-year-old was found dead to Ireland after her uncontrolled rage consumed her in a hate-filled rant against the small independent state and its citizens, who in turn gave as good as they got.

Ms Banks, who was physically and psychologically abused as a child by a mother who loved to call her ugly, ironically died after mirroring her parent, calling Irish women 'fat and ugly'.

Health and fitness tip

HIIT stands for 'High-Intensity Intestinal Trauma'.

'Azealia's own deep-down resentment for herself was triggered by a series of unfortunate events which eventually left her dead to Ireland,' a pathologist for the thin-skinned star explained. 'We believe a defence mechanism kicked in and triggered some form of self-loathing, which in turn was aimed at the unprepared nation by the rapper.

'Unfortunately, Ms Banks was unaware of how good the Irish also are at being verbally abusive. The end result left her completely dead to her tens of fans here and, of course, the entire population,' he added.

Banks, best known for that one track she had with music someone else wrote, is to be removed from the Irish psyche later this week, before being buried in a mass of social-media feeds containing

vicious sentiments about her race and looks.

The 'artist' leaves behind two mixtapes, one underperforming album, and a questionable Instagram account.

TELEVISION

HOW WOULD THE 1916 LEADERS FARE ON *TAKE ME OUT*?

Let the Casement see the basement! Wildly popular dating TV show *Take Me Out* continues to garner new fans who love the idea of one man being put in front of 30 eligible ladies to fight over. But the question which has been on everybody's lips remains – how would our beloved 1916 leaders fare on the ITV show fronted by Paddy McGuinness? Let's see:

Pádraig Pearse

The contestants would initially butcher the pronunciation of his name but would warm to a man who is obviously very passionate, with Paddy insisting on calling him 'Pad Rag'.

Our experts conservatively estimate he would still have 20 out of 30 lights after the first round. Not many people are aware of this but Pádraig had a very noticeable squint, which the *Take Me Out* women would pretend not to silently judge him about.

Pádraig, off to a good start, would dramatically lose a further 19 lights after the ladies learned how important his Catholic faith was to him in the second round, which heard from interviews with those closest to him.

Round three – the talent round – would see Pádraig dressed in full military regalia quoting from the Proclamation. All lights out from there, sadly.

Roger Casement

Roger would benefit from the fact that he looks like the result of a scientific experiment which sought to create the perfect hipster. With that stand-out facial hair, he would keep 30 for 30 in the first round, with no lady turning off her light.

News of the fact he was widely travelled, with time spent in the Congo and Brazil, would put off plenty of women who don't like the idea of their partner being away for long periods of time cataloguing the crimes of King Leopold II of Belgium, thus reducing his options to 12.

However, after then learning of his gunning past, many women would regret turning off their lights. Roger would likely be matched with Tegan, an Instagram influencer from Bradford.

James Connolly

Due to his Scottish brogue, James would initially be a big hit with the ladies, but once there was mention of him having kids and his belief that wealthy people should be heavily taxed, the 30 women wouldn't be able to hit off their lights fast enough.

Thomas Clarke

A silver fox, Tom would intrigue the ladies at first with his gentrified and mannerly ways, his Tyrone accent winning over plenty of them.

However, being a member of the Irish Republican Brotherhood, an organisation banned by the English government, wouldn't sit well with the ladies on *Take Me Out*, and poor Tom would head home without securing a trip to Fernandos.

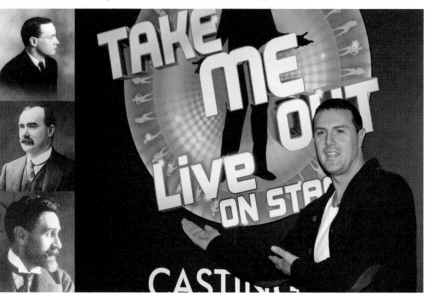

MUSIC

MALE SINGERS NOW ALL SINGING WITH THAT SAME ANNOYING WHINE

A NEW study of male singer-songwriters and band lead singers has revealed that, to the untrained ear, they all sound like one single individual with a particularly grating, whiny voice which could drive anyone insane.

While the over-earnest, pleading vocal delivery of confessional pop/indie/R&B songs has been ever-

'When one song is listened to in isolation, it seems harmless enough'

present for over 20 years, the high level of 'whininess' is only a recent phenomenon.

'We're working on it and we're sorry for the mental anguish caused by the horrific whining,' confirmed a senior Spotify official, who is aware of the increase of people smashing their phones and music players upon being subjected to the whining again and again and again.

Conspiracy theorists claim that the singer from The Chainsmokers has been cloned and is now posing as 40,000 other bands and singers, including several inexplicably popular ones here in Ireland.

'When one song is listened to in isolation, it seems harmless enough, and can even provoke a lasting emotional connection to the song for a listener, but the problem is the next 100 songs from male artists with too many feelings have the exact same insufferable wailing, all trying to sound so genuine and in the moment that you just vomit on the spot upon hearing it,' confirmed one music scientist.

Experts would not reveal the specific artists and bands guilty of the offensive and irritable whine, opting instead to simply state, 'You've a fucking radio, don't you?'

Despite the troubling news, radio DJs remain infuriatingly upbeat about the whole thing.

Community text alerts

Foreign lad in number 18 still messing with that car, whatever he's bloody at. Four Saturdays in a row now and it still sounds like a tractor driving in a Pringles tube.

MOVIES

SO CUTE: CHECK OUT WHAT THE FACEHUGGER FROM THE ORIGINAL *ALIEN* MOVIE LOOKS LIKE TODAY

HE was the adorable little tyke that launched a million plush cuddly toys, and which outsold ET figurines in the 1980s, but what does the lovable Facehugger from *Alien* look like today? You'd be shocked!

Read on to have your mind well and truly blown.

Woah! No, you're not seeing things. This Facehugger has been hugging the weights and looks buff AF! What a stone-cold fox, and no, you're not dreaming. He really does spit acid from his mouth. Young Facehugger probably wore braces on his face when going through his awkward teenager phase, but boy has it paid off. He's all grown up with his metallic teeth, which are to die for.

The keen-eyed among you will have noticed he has teeth for days!

Nice to see he still has that same twinkle in what we only presume are his eyes.

Suburban Dictionary

'Sure, this is it': What 'this' is, and why it is 'it', remains unsolved by the greatest thinkers of our age.

WWN Was There

Waterford Whispers News

Fianna Fáil government illegally taps journalists' phones, November 1982

What we said then: Fuck the journalists, they're the competition.

What we say now: Fuck those journalists, they were the competition.

MOVIES

BIT WHERE EMMA THOMPSON DOESN'T GET NECKLACE STILL BREAKS LOCAL MAN'S HEART

WATERFORD native Kenneth Farraher has reluctantly completed his mandatory annual watch of festive favourite *Love, Actually* with his wife Marie, during which time he mocked and derided most of the movie's soppy love stories – apart from that scene where Emma Thompson found out Alan Rickman was cheating on her and she went up to her room and cried, because she didn't deserve that. Damn it, she didn't deserve that.

Farraher, 34, has had to suffer through an annual watch of the 2003 romcom with his then-girlfriend, now-wife Marie for the past ten years. He manages to maintain a gruff Can't-Be-Bothered-With-This-Shit demeanour throughout the 135 minutes of interlacing stories of love and loss between wealthy, famous English people, chipping in with comments about how the lad from *The Walking*

> **'He hasn't a clue that she knows everything, and that he's been caught'**

Dead is a 'sneaky cunt' for hitting on his friend's wife like that.

However, Farraher's demeanour changes when Karen, played by Emma Thompson, receives a gift from her husband Harry, played by Hans Gruber, which is a tell-tale sign he has been having an affair behind her back, prompting the Waterford man to excuse himself to the kitchen to 'make tea' and have a bit of a sob.

'Just … just how she knows she has to hold it together, for the sake of her kids at Christmas,' sobbed Farraher, pretending to look for crisps in the

kitchen until the redness of his eyes died down.

'And Harry, the fucking prick, he hasn't a clue that she knows everything, and that he's been caught. How could someone be so clueless? How could someone be so cruel, to the mother of their children? At Christmas? And for what? Some bit of strange in the office? Harry, how could you do this? I'll tell you one thing, Emma Thompson, you're better off without him!'

Farraher went on to compose himself before heading back in to catch the finale of the movie, where he could cover up his tender side with a series of jokes about how Liam Neeson's son should have been shot while running through airport security in a post-9/11 world.

Fullmindness

It's easy to go off on a negative tangent of thoughts before going asleep. A great way to reverse this is by drinking large amounts of alcohol before bedtime and swallowing four to five Valium.

MUSIC

CHRISTY MOORE OPENS EYES FOR FIRST TIME IN 30 YEARS FOLLOWING SURGERY

LEGENDARY singer-songwriter Christy Moore caught a glimpse of the world around him for the first time in over 30 years, following a revolutionary surgical procedure that pried open his tightly shut eyelids.

Christy Moore, born Christy Moore, has suffered from a rare optical condition called squintivitis since hitting the big time with Planxty back in the mid-70s. Brought on from years of banging out emotionally charged folk songs, the condition had left the Kildare-born crooner almost 100 per cent blind, until the intervention of this radical new surgery.

Moore went under the knife last weekend, and shared an emotional moment with his family this morning when the bandages finally came off and a 20/20

field of vision was returned to the 'Ride On' singer.

'Mr Moore has responded very well to the procedure, and is sitting up eating rice grain by grain at the moment,' said Dr Ian Seawell, Head of Optometry in the Mater Hospital.

'When he came in here last week, he looked like he was wincing all the time, like he'd just stubbed his toe while getting out of bed. But now look at him: big, bulbous eyes just sticking out there. It's … an odd look for anyone familiar with Christy, to be honest. He sang us "Ordinary Man" earlier today and, well, I won't lie … It looked fucking weird.'

With the eye surgery a success, Moore will now undergo a procedure to unclench his jaw for the first time since the mid-90s.

Veteran journalist Bill Badbody takes a leave of absence from his day-to-day reporting at WWN HQ to pursue a career in politics, in the hope of securing a place as MEP in the European elections. This is his story.

Week 6

Missed Darkness Into Light march. Got to stop watching Nazi docs on History Channel late at night. Sent Fiachra to the photo shop again to make it look like I was walking with everyone this morning. Everyone on the mental-health bandwagon these days. Got Fiachra to open up about my depression online. Posted 'I was sad once'. Boom! 20k likes. Hopefully *The Late Late Show* gets wind and invites me on.

Need to do more to get attention and press. Going to borrow my good friend Peter Casey's line and rant about the Travelling community. Suppose it's not important to mean it or believe it, just important to get the media coverage and a handy few votes.

Told crowds of voters today that 'You can't say anything these days as Leo and the EU's PC-gone-mad globalists have banned free speech'. They all cheered. Proceeded to list all the things you can't say any more. Will be on several national radio stations later to recite list and explain how you can't say anything these days.

Spotted a really weird thing on the new house cameras: Javier and Anne were in the sitting room on the floor. Javier seemed to be doing push-ups over Anne, or maybe Anne was doing press-ups using Javier. I couldn't make it out because the coffee table was in the way, but Javier is way too heavy for her to be doing press-ups with. Need to have a word. She'll put her back out, the silly mare.

Horrified to find a big black dog urinating on my car wheel after the valet this morning. Told the owner to clean it up and he wouldn't. Gardaí wouldn't even listen to me on the phone. Checked Google and no law in place to clean up pet urine. Will campaign for compulsory urine sponges for dog owners.

Still annoyed about the final season of *Game of Thrones*: Everyone else has moved on but I still want to moan and moan and moan about the last season, but now people are slagging me and telling to get a life and that it's 'only a TV show'. Need someone who is as similarly petty and negative as myself, and willing to while away hours of their life complaining, going around in circles, and making piss-poor points.

Call Keith on 085 0915 2857.

MUSIC

'I'M SELF-TAUGHT,' REVEALS TAMBOURINIST LIAM GALLAGHER

BRITISH tambourinist Liam Gallagher has revealed that he has spent decades mastering his musical instrument of choice without ever receiving any lessons from an outside source, stating that being 'self-taught' is the key to his stunning success.

In a tell-all interview with WWN, Mr Gallagher said he used to 'tap desks' in school with his fingers, before progressing to shaking restaurant salt shakers in his mid-teens.

'At that time, it was all fucking guitar wank this, piano pansy that,' Liam recalled of his time growing up in Manchester as a struggling musician. 'I always thought that mainstream shit

'Noel's a daft, jealous cunt and a fucking Bono-lick-arse ponce'

was too easy, ya know? Not for me, our kid.'

Liam's first memory of picking up the tambourine was when he was just 15 years old, wowing peers and budding musicians alike with his unique, over-the-head shaking style.

'Noel and his mates were practising one day, playing a riff, and

without thinking I just picked up the tambourine and started shaking it over me head,' the 46-year-old went on. 'Noel said I was right good and had a natural talent for shaking shit, innit?'

The Oasis frontman went on in detail about his rigorous tambourine practise routine, which sometimes interfered with his academic studies.

'I used to doss off school an' that and shake all day,' he recalled. 'I'd shake so much that I had one hand bigger than the other. All the other kids in school would slag me off for being a wanking cunt. That's when I started hiding my hands behind my back when performing.'

It wasn't until late 1995 when Liam realised there could be a career ahead of him as a professional tambourinist.

'Bob Dylan's song "Mr Tambourine Man" was a huge inspiration to me. All my life I just wanted to be the best tambourine man that ever lived, and when "Wonderwall" hit, I knew that it was tambourine time and that I was on to something truly fucking special,' he said.

'The whole country just kept going on about how good I was on tambourine, and things just really took off for the band from there.'

Oasis went from strength to strength and soon became known as the world's number-one tambourine band. However, after years of internal feuding and jealous behaviour from brother Noel, Liam knew that Oasis's time was over.

'Noel was always envious of my tambourine playing. I think that's what really drove us apart,' Liam revealed, now caressing a tambourine in his hand. 'If I had the chance to go back in time, I wouldn't change a fucking thing. Fucking tosser.

'Noel's a daft, jealous cunt and a fucking Bono-lick-arse ponce anyway,' Liam concluded.

KARL LAGERFELD'S COFFIN LOOKING KINDA FAT TO US

WWN Fashion has joined our industry brothers and sisters in mourning this week, following the death of Karl Lagerfeld, currently laid out in a shroud that does nothing for his profile, if we're being perfectly honest.

Karl, probably the best Lagerfeld in the world, passed away this week after 60 years in the fashion industry, during which time he captured the world's imagination with his designs, while letting fatties know their place, which is why it's such a shame that his current coffin just looks so … puffy.

Health and fitness tip

Bookmark your favourite takeaways in your web browser. It saves you a lot of time in the long run.

> **'We've ordered him to lose 20lbs immediately so we can squeeze him into a smaller coffin'**

Vocally critical of migrants, the #MeToo movement, Adele, women who aren't a size zero, and women in general, the 85-year-old has left a sizable hole in the fashion industry, as well as a sizeable hole that needs digging in the cemetery.

'We don't really feel comfortable sending Karl out like this, so we've ordered him to lose 20lbs immediately so we can squeeze him into a smaller coffin,' said a close family friend.

'It's what he would have wanted. He spent his entire professional life berating women for their size, so it's only right that he lead by example and shed some weight before the big day. Look at that coffin. It'd take 50 catwalk models to carry it, although in fairness, they're weak from not eating so that they could match his standard for the industry.'

UPDATE: To avoid fat-coffin embarrassment, Lagerfeld is now to be cremated and his ashes kept in a barrel.

GAMING

VIDEO GAME DEVELOPER GIVES FEMALE CHARACTER MASSIVE BREASTS AND TINY WAIST, FOR A CHANGE

A VIDEO game developer has fought the urge to conform to the realistic demands placed on representing the female form in video games, bravely giving his characters massive breasts and a tiny waist.

Community text alerts

The Wilsons will be getting a skip next weekend for their renovations. If you have any mattresses you'd like to get rid of under the cover of darkness, now's the time.

The Khaladeen Prophecies, a role-playing game due out early next year, has excited fans of similar, fantasy-tinged fare with vast worlds to explore. However, lead character artist Gary Lauer has avoided the expectations heaped on him to design the main female protagonist, Lauritha Sengwen of Dolth, in such a way that she resembles an actual human woman.

'I decided to go against the grain and do something truly revolutionary for a game. I gave my female character massive boobs and one of those waists that, if she were real, would mean that she would die,

because there'd be no room for the vital organs,' explained Lauer.

The quest-heavy game sees Lauritha and her sworn protector, Nuneenth the Brave, traipse the globe in search of treasure foretold in the Khaladeen prophecies, something Lauer is immensely proud of.

'So basically, we make her run around a lot. I mean, that's like all she does … But it's cool, 'cos you see her breasts flop up and down,' confirmed Lauer, who doesn't get out much.

Activision Blizzard, distributors of the hugely anticipated title, have confirmed the unrealistic composition of the female heroine is a huge step forward in female representation in games, as it gives teenage boys yet another thing to fantasise about at length while alone in their bedrooms.

UPDATE: After intense criticism on forums from fans, Lauer has revised the character's body to allow for a larger, rounder bottom.

TELEVISION

EVERY MURDER TO HAVE ITS OWN NETFLIX DOCUMENTARY BY 2025

STATISTICIANS have revealed that if Netflix keeps up its current rate of producing documentaries on lurid killings, they will run out of murders to make shows about by 2025.

Every known murder logged and investigated by police around the world is currently in the process of being churned out by Netflix, weaving these salacious tales of violence and horror into one-off films or gripping eight-part series.

'It's unclear if, by 2025, Netflix will just have to play the waiting game and wait for new murders to occur, or if they themselves will turn to killing people in order to fuel that strange, twisted desire the public has for shows about murderers,' confirmed one statistician we spoke with.

The average Netflix viewer usually scrolls through the service for hours on end, pretending to be interested in the 'sciency documentaries', before diving into a relaxing eight-hour documentary about a man who murdered his granny, assumed her identity and then killed everyone in her nursing home.

'We're not judging Netflix for it. I suppose it's a nice thing. In the middle of being murdered, you can comfort yourself with the thought of your own face filling one of the those Netflix tiles on the homepage,' added the statistician.

Speculation is rife as to where else Netflix could turn to for televisual content should every murder be covered by 2025, with some subscribers offering up suggestions.

'More murders, more murders, more murders,' confirmed the angry mob outside Netflix's offices, demanding the supply of crime documentaries never cease.

LAUGHING COW OPENS UP ABOUT DEPRESSION

'PEOPLE don't want to associate sadness and spreadable cheese. They want happiness with every foil-wrapped triangle, and that's ... that's where I come in,' explained the Laughing Cow as she flashed us that classic, broad bovine grin that we know from our childhood, all the while a glint of poignancy shining in her big eyes.

In an intimate, tell-all exclusive interview with WWN, the Laughing Cow (or 'La vache qui rit', to give her her native French title) opened up about her introduction to the world of lunchables, her battle with depression, and her new life as an ambassador for sad heifers across the world.

'I was ... maybe six months on the pasture when word came around that this company was looking for a fun-loving cow to represent their brand,' said the Laughing Cow, chewing slowly.

'I thought, what the hell, why not? So I auditioned. It turned out that I had the right combination of winning smile, friendly demeanour, and the fucking bright red skin they were looking for. They stuck a pair of cheese-carton earrings on me, and the next thing I knew I was an international superstar.'

Although rarely pictured without her trademark grin, the Laughing Cow admitted that life hadn't been all crackers and grapes.

'You have to know that it's okay to not be okay, and to reach out when you're udder the weather,' said the Laughing Cow, who asked us to refer to her as just 'the Cow' when the cameras weren't rolling.

'I'm okay most days, but then I think about how I may have led other young calves astray. They see me on the tubs, grinning away, and they aspire to be like me. They change their bodies to be like me. They spend hours practising their smiles. All the while, men are taking advantage of them. These poor cows think they're going to be models, but they just want them for their milk. It's hard not to feel responsible for that. It really mooooves me to tears.'

The Laughing Cow also told us that she had begun to see a cow therapist, who is an expert in his field.

EXCLUSIVE

MARTY MORRISSEY LAUNCHES BRANDED LINE OF SEX TOYS IN TIME FOR CHRISTMAS

CONSIDER Christmas presents for the family sorted now that RTÉ presenting ace Marty Morrissey has released his new branded line of sex toys in time for the festive season.

The 2019 Marty Morrissey Masturbatory Collection for Self-Satisfaction, or MMMCSS for short, is a direct follow-up to the wildly popular 2018 range, and Marty has once again partnered

'It's funny, when testing the MMMCSS collection, that's exactly the sound women and men made when putting on the nipple clamps'

up with leading Japanese sex-toy manufacturer Sexaguru.

The MorriGee Dildo is set to be this festive season's bestseller, with Marty's face emblazoned on the business end of the pleasuring device, retailing at a reasonable €29.99.

'We're all about quality and customer satisfaction,' confirmed Haruto Kagawa, the man tasked with bringing Marty's designs and sexual appeal to life.

'It's funny, when testing the MMMCSS collection, that's exactly the sound women and men made when putting on the nipple clamps and what have you for a test drive: "mmmcss",' added Kagawa.

The MMMCSS line, which contains two unique dildo designs, nine vibrators of different sizes, poppers, sex swings and Fleshlights, all based on Marty's likeness, goes on sale at midnight tonight.

To avoid a repeat of last year's riots after supplies ran low, some 300,000 sex toys have been delivered in the first of ten batches destined for Ireland between now and Christmas.

Inside the Mind of a Nightclub Bouncer

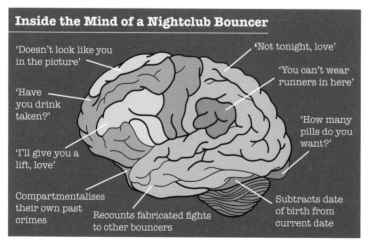

'Doesn't look like you in the picture'

'Have you drink taken?'

'I'll give you a lift, love'

Compartmentalises their own past crimes

Recounts fabricated fights to other bouncers

'Not tonight, love'

'You can't wear runners in here'

'How many pills do you want?'

Subtracts date of birth from current date

BREAKING NEWS

PRESIDENT ATTENDS FIFTH ANNIVERSARY OF GARTH BROOKS SAGA

COMMEMORATIONS are underway to mark the fifth anniversary of the cancelled Garth Brooks concerts at Croke Park, which caused outrage among hundreds of thousands of ticket holders in 2014.

Laying a wreath at Croke Park, and wiping a tear from his eye, President Michael D Higgins said there was much to learn from the mistakes of the past, and learn we must.

'The events of 2014 live long in the memory and will never be forgotten,' the president said from a plinth outside Croke Park, his voice carrying across the heads of the thousands in attendance.

The discord caused by the objections to the concerts, and Brooks' subsequent cancellation of all dates, plunged Ireland into a whirlpool of invective-dominated debate and violence. One riot saw Croke Park residents clash with cowboy-hat-wearing culchies. Fourteen people died.

Later, medical professionals would confirm that the Irish public suffered something akin to a collective mental breakdown under the weight of the constant Garth-Brooks-focused news cycles.

'It is the saddest chapter in Ireland's history. I recall an advertisement placed in the local paper after the gigs were cancelled. It brings a tear to my eye again today, as it did when I first read it. "For sale: cowboy boots, never worn",' continued the president, drawing loud, grief-stricken wailing from the crowd.

The president will later host a reception in the Phoenix Park for victims – concert ticket holders – and tomorrow morning he will attend the opening of the Garth Brooks Centre for Peaceful Planning of Large-Scale Concerts.

It is hoped that the centre can be used in the event of any future resident–concert promoter disagreements, with many music fans already trying to book the centre in order to get Picture This at the 3Arena cancelled, and The Coronas deported to a soundproofed island off the coast of Iceland.

Fullmindness

Remember to slow down. Walk around work like you're in slow motion – all the time. Reply with slow-motion responses when asked questions. Do as little as humanly possible. Blame your self-diagnosed anxiety on all your failings and kiss your stress goodbye.

MUSIC

TWENTY-three years after the Spice Girls burst into our lives with their smash hit single 'Wannabe', a sensational new book penned by band member Mel B has revealed the actual meaning behind the lyrics 'Zig-a-Zig-ah'.

Melanie Brown, in no way motivated to stir controversy because she has a book to sell and a Spice Girls tour to promote, hinted the phrase was

'ZIG-A-ZIG-AH' REVEALED TO BE CUNNILINGUS

something herself and fellow band member Geri Halliwell came up with one night while experimenting with their lady parts.

During a clip from a recent interview with Britain's favourite phone-tapping tabloid editor, Piers Morgan, the 44-year-

old adult confessed to having lesbian sex with her then-bandmate, in the hopes that this kind of thing still makes the news, much to her publisher's delight.

'"Zig-a-Zig-ah" was the noise we made when, you know …' Mel B teased

'If you wanna be my lover, you gotta go down on my friends'

reluctant viewers, before further ruining the song. 'If you wanna be my lover, you gotta go down on my friends.'

Following the news, shares in Girl Power soared by 43 per cent during morning trading, with Google also reporting a spike in search terms from middle-aged men looking for an answer to the question: 'How can women be bisexual if they are married to a man?'

Meanwhile, the lesbian community has issued an open letter on the PR stunt, stating: 'Thanks for using our sexuality to get a few column inches in the papers, you absolute fucking dose.'

RTÉ RUNNING OUT OF THINGS FOR 'CELEBRITIES' TO DO

'I'M telling you now, we're not putting a fucking skating rink into the Helix,' said RTÉ director general Dee Forbes, shooting down the idea that the national broadcaster was about to commission its own version of *Dancing On Ice*, at a think-tank meeting aimed at finding something for the nation's celebrities to do.

'Find something for Jennifer Zamparelli, Lar

Corbett and Fionnuala from *Glenroe* to do that we can do in Studio One for less than sixty grand an episode, or you're all fired,' she shouted.

Forbes' outburst comes as creative chiefs at RTÉ admitted that after celebrity-based shows about cooking, dancing, living on a farm, singing, more dancing, and managing small GAA teams, they're currently out

of workable ideas for the nation's most affordable stars.

'Celebrity Stop-Sign Men,' pitched one creative, sweating bullets in the high-stakes meeting.

'We get Simon Delaney to work for the council for a week,' he continued. 'Or *Celebrity Air Stewards*? Get Nadia Forde in a Ryanair outfit, asking everyone if they want to buy scratch cards. *Celebrity ... Celebrity Teachers*! *Celebrity IRA*? Marty Morrissey in a balaclava that only comes down to his top lip. *Celebrity Celebrities*.

Just a load of celebrities in the RTÉ canteen fighting to the death to be on *The Late Late Show*. *Celebrity Drug Mules*. *Celebrity Knife Fights*. *The Chase*, but with celebrities! I know a lad who works in ITV. He'd sell us the set for ten grand, tops. *Celebrity Sweatshops*. Fuck ... *Celebrity Cooking*? Like *Masterchef*, but ... well, no, just like *Masterchef*.'

The nation's celebrities currently await the outcome of the meeting, knowing their very livelihoods depend on *Celebs Go to Direct Provision* getting the green light.

TELEVISION

THE SIMPSONS RENEWED UNTIL ALL LIFE ON EARTH EXTINGUISHED

20TH Century Fox has confirmed that *The Simpsons* has been renewed not just for a record-breaking 31st and 32nd season, but, with that, the long-running show has been renewed for the rest of time: until the seas boil; until the air has disappeared into the cold blankness of space; until man is nothing more than a memory floating among the stars.

The news comes as no shock to anyone, following 30 years of adventures and escapades with the Simpson family, during which time the show has gone from a hilarious, gold-standard comedy programme, to a well-drawn animation in the correct aspect ratio, if nothing else.

Doubts had been floated following contract disputes with key members of the cast, but Fox is confident that, after 30 years, they now have instances of Marge, Homer, Lisa, Bart and the rest of the gang mentioning every single word in the English language at least once, allowing them to splice together enough dialogue to create new episodes until whatever holocaust awaits humanity down the road.

'When the Earth lies silent, broken and ruined, we'll still be churning out episodes of *The Simpsons*,' beamed the corpse of Matt Groening, momentarily brought back to life by jags of electricity from copper probes attached to his temples.

'Nestled in a bunker, deep underground, our algorithm will spit forth season 389 with new adventures in Springfield, for endless hours of yellow-tinged, D'oh!-filled madness. There won't be anyone around to watch them, but fuck it, that's not stopping us now.'

Meanwhile, fresh *Simpsons* merchandise will hit the shops soon, so if you haven't bought yourself a Duff Beer bottle opener or an 'Ay, Caramba!' alarm clock, now's your chance.

Community text alerts

Michael Roche making a hames of reversing his car out of the drive. He's now asking the neighbour across the way to move their car out of his way. You could turn a bus there.

MOVIES

WHAT'S THE RIGHT AGE TO INTRODUCE YOUR KIDS TO *GOODFELLAS?*

MARTIN Scorsese's ultra-violent and profane gangster classic is a masterpiece, of that there is no doubt. However, the question can arise for parents who want to introduce their children to one of the greatest movies of the last 30 years: When is 'too young' to sit them down in front of *GoodFellas*?

In a bid to help answer that question, we sat some toddlers down to watch Ray Liotta get coked out of his mind and a little paranoid.

Our cute little volunteers – Seán, 3; Amy, 3 and a half; and Daisy, 36 months (her mother seemed incapable of counting in years) – took their places in front of a 70-inch screen with surround sound, and we pressed play.

Minute 2: Incapable of sitting still and, frankly, showing no respect for the craft of film-making. We strapped them to the chairs and kept their eyes open with Sellotape.

Minute 17: Crying like the little babies they are. We told them to just shush and wait, *Frozen* will be starting any minute. That seemed to calm them down.

Minute 55: The flinching and startling jolts each toddler made as successive gangster hits and beat downs were handed out proved conclusively what we all know – Scorsese's movie is not a celebration of violence, more a stark reminder of how reprehensibly people can act.

Minute 59: Had to turn up the volume again because the crying was drowning out Joe Pesci calling people cunts.

Minute 81: Seán has soiled himself. Was it the trauma of watching this movie or a regular bowel movement? Too early to tell.

Minute 109: The three kids are really connecting with the movie. Their readily flowing tears and cries for 'Mama' and 'Dada' reflect Liotta's Henry Hill character's loss of innocence.

Minute 112: Holy shit, Robert De Niro wasted a whole bunch of people in this movie. Completely forgot how good some of the deaths are in this. Quick, rewind that bit. I want to watch it again.

Minute 145: Man, you can see the bits of Joe Pesci's brains fly out of his skull when he's shot in the head. The practical effects in this were top-fucking-notch. All three kids shivering now, with empty, haunted looks on their faces.

Conclusion: You need to watch this movie at least once a year. It's so fucking good. Use the kids as an excuse.

ww news

Waterford Whispers News

LIFESTYLE

RELATIONSHIPS

A well-known local 'Basic Bitch' has had her status upgraded to 'Premium Bitch' after expressing an interest in a series of exciting and diverse activities. Karen Kilty, 26, had been labelled a so-called 'Basic Bitch' due to her fondness for unoriginal and uninteresting fashion, music, movies and hobbies, each of which would spark someone to say, 'Of course

'BASIC BITCH' UPGRADED TO 'PREMIUM BITCH'

Karen likes Taylor Swift, she's such a basic bitch'.

Kilty confirmed she is no longer the most basic of bitches after taking some bold leaps in recent weeks, developing a refined taste for fringe cultural happenings, resulting in the achievement of 'Premium Bitch' status.

'Karen used to play it safe. She'd be in bed at 9 p.m. each night, only ever drank a white-wine spritzer, never tried any exotic food. She'd only ever watch *Grey's Anatomy*, but that's all changed,' confirmed one long-time friend, Jessica.

Kilty's transformation has seen her denounce Beyoncé in favour of the more artistically relevant Solange, while slowly becoming an expert on Caribbean cuisine and the films of Europe's leading LGBT filmmakers.

'There was a time where she'd just watch *Corrie*. Now it's all "I'm doing a triathlon in an active volcano and off to a BDSM swingers' club afterwards." I don't recognise her,' added Jessica.

Suburban Dictionary

'**Culchie**': A term of great endearment for a simple-minded, backwards rural type who can't seem to take praise or a compliment.

WWN Was There

𝔚aterford 𝔚hispers News

Roy Keane leaves Saipan before the start of the World Cup, May 2002

What we said then: The FAI is a joke, a disgrace of an organisation. What it needs know is the steady hand of John Delaney to drag it kicking and screaming into the 21st century. With him at the helm, we can kiss goodbye to embarrassing episodes like this and wave a fond farewell to the nod-and-a-wink culture.

What we say now: I was actually out sick that day, so obviously I have no idea who wrote this endorsement of Mr Delaney. It certainly wasn't me, and you can't prove otherwise.

MOTORING

CHICKENSHIT STANDS OUTSIDE HIS CAR DURING AUTOMATIC WASH

AN absolute chickenshit was caught standing outside his own car while it was being washed by an automatic washing machine at a local garage, WWN can confirm.

The man, who eye-witnesses believe was in his early to late forties, purchased the car wash at approximately 3 p.m. from a member of staff, drove his car carefully into the automatic car wash, and then ignored the signs that he should remain inside the vehicle.

'The sick bastard just opened his driver's door and made his way over to the code panel and proceeded to type in his wash code,' one man who was getting petrol at the time recalled. 'Everyone was wondering what the hell he was doing. It was actually embarrassing to watch.'

Staff at the garage stated that 'normal motorists' are supposed to stop at the code panel while still in the car. The green light prompts the driver forward, with the red light appearing when they need to stop.

It is understood the man simply just stared at his car while it was being washed, while other customers

> **'The sick bastard just opened his driver's door and made his way over to the code panel and proceeded to type in his wash code'**

and staff stared at him, wondering what kind of individual he was at all.

'He was obviously too scared to stay in the car while it was being washed,' a member of staff explained. 'We get chickenshits like that in here all the time.'

DINING

'IS Barry on tonight?' began middle-aged customer Margaret Caulfield, who spent her first three minutes in busy Waterford city restaurant the Coddle Pot frantically looking for attention. 'Barry's usually on Friday nights. Is he off?'

Immediately discerning the woman's particular customer persona as one they were reluctantly well-versed in, staff drew plastic straws to see who would look after the dreaded table 15.

'He must be still out golfing. He was saying he was going out golfing the last day I was in. He's always golfing, that Barry. Is he on later at

ARSEHOLE CUSTOMER 'KNOWS THE OWNER'

all?' Mrs Caulfield repeated again to herself, now slightly less frantic due to the sudden appearance of waiter Darius Flak, who was anxiously squeezing his short straw for dear life behind his back.

'Hello, and welcome to the Coddle Pot. My name is Darius. Would you like to see the menu?' he asked, blissfully ignoring the woman's calls for the owner, knowing the cunning ruse for getting preferential treatment all too well.

'Barry, is he on tonight? I don't see him on,' she persisted, now squinting behind the waiter as though he were invisible. 'I could have sworn I heard him there when I came in.'

'I'm sorry, I don't actually know. Can I help you with your order?' the waiter asked.

'I suppose I'll go for my usual, then,' the daughter-of-two scoffed, staring vacantly at him.

'And that would be?' he replied.

> **'Can I have one hake special, please, for this dose on table 15 who apparently knows the owner Gary, but for some reason insists on calling him Barry'**

'If Barry was here now he'd know what that was … Anyway, give me the hake special you have on there. It's very disappointing Barry isn't here,' she ordered, before the waiter went back to the kitchen.

'Can I have one hake special, please, for this dose on table 15 who apparently knows the owner Gary, but for some reason insists on calling him Barry,' the waiter told the chef, giving him a 'one of those cunts' smile and a nod.

BREAKING NEWS

79 PER CENT OF PARENTS DON'T WANT YOU HANGING OUT WITH THAT SINÉAD ONE AGAIN

REPORTS coming in this morning suggest that as many as 79 per cent of concerned and overbearing parents do not want you 'hanging out with that Sinéad one again'.

Citing carefully gathered research which concluded 'Because I said so', and 'I don't like the look of her', parents were wary of Sinéad's ability to put thoughts into your head and ultimately lead you astray.

'We had no idea of this Sinéad one's magical ability to transport her thoughts directly into the minds of others,' shared parenting expert Dr Emily von Strood, shocked by the news. 'How she does this is unclear, but it could be by accessing the hole in people's ears somehow and inserting thoughts directly to the brain. This warrants more investigation and research.'

'That Sinéad one' was unavailable for comment as she is believed by parents to be hanging out around the back of a shop, injecting cannabis into her eyeballs while inventing new, previously unheard of swearwords.

The 79 per cent of parents ordering you not to hang out with Sinéad deny they are overreacting, defending their completely reasonable position by warning that 'Sinéad might appear cool right now, but just give it a few years and you'll soon realise.'

Unconfirmed claims by 79 per cent of parents also suggest that long-term friendship with Sinéad can lead to party attendance, drinking, smoking, orgies and – worst of all – an increase in talking back to your parents.

IRISH model and general woman-person Glenda O'Connorman Roche received floods of praise on social media yesterday afternoon for showing off her water wrinkles following a four-hour bath.

The 25-year-old Miss Solar System contestant posted several unedited images of her fingertips, which seemed to have shrivelled up due to her blood vessels constricting below the skin on her hands and feet.

Despite initially posting about the wrinkles as if they were an actual problem, O'Connorman Roche went on to insist that they weren't a problem. She just wanted to post the pictures anyway in case someone did have a problem with them. 'Water wrinkles

MODEL PRAISED FOR BARING WRINKLY FINGERS AFTER LONG BATH

are 100 per cent natural and nothing to be ashamed of, so I'm just making sure everyone knows that fact,' she wrote.

'At the end of the day, I'm just like you ordinary people who get out of the bath with water wrinkles and take pictures of them. I want to highlight them as a natural attribute of the female human body and nothing to frown upon, even though they look kind of weird. But yeah, I'm sure they'll dry out and be gone in no time.'

It didn't take long for fans to praise the daughter-of-two for her inspirational bravery.

'I'm so influenced by this I just had a bath,' one happy fan commented. 'I wish these water wrinkles would just stay for ever – I love them now!'

Since her post, the model has released a water wrinkle cream, which will keep the blood vessels constricted for up to five hours at a time.

'Such was the praise for them, I decided to release a cream that lets you prolong your water wrinkles. This cream will allow you to flaunt your water wrinkles on a night out and will help shoot down any water wrinkle shamers out there,' the model stated.

Glenda O'Connorman Roche's new cream is on sale for €199 in all good cosmetic stores.

FASHION

FUCK ALL STARS TURN OUT FOR WATERFORD FASHION WEEK

WATERFORD Fashion Week 2019 wrapped up yesterday after just two days, following a catwalk exhibition of Ben Sherman shirts, knock-off Hilfiger stuff from the markets, and whatever you can get in TK Maxx for 20 quid or less.

The dull event attracted literally nobody from the world of fashion or art, with not even a *Tallafornia* reject or social media influencer showing up to the glitz-free bash, despite all the free Tuborg and ham sandwiches on offer.

Although invites were extended to fashion luminaries such as Marty

Health and fitness tip

Drinking one tiny, overpriced probiotic a day will permanently undo years of bad meal, drink and drug choices.

> ## If London, New York and Paris can have fashion weeks, then there's no reason Waterford can't

Morrisey, the *Xposé* girls and radio DJ Niall Boylan, in the end the event had to make do with one photographer taking shots in portrait on his iPhone, while local designer Cáit Lennon showcased her new portfolio, St Vincent de Paul's half-price bin.

'Perhaps Waterford doesn't really need a fashion week,' mused Lennon, widely regarded as a tax on the patience.

TV guide

The Taoiseach's Socks: An exclusive, all-access, behind-the-scenes, backstage-pass, past-the-velvet-rope look at Leo Varadkar's sock collection. The hard-hitting interview, conducted by Ryan Tubridy, will see Varadkar asked how much he likes socks, and which would be his favourite, if he had to choose one pair.

Friday, 8 p.m., RTÉ One.

'No, actually, you know what? I won't hear of it. If London, New York and Paris can have fashion weeks, then there's no reason Waterford can't. Everyone just needs to get more into fashion, and what it means to the world. Look, there's a boy wearing a hoodie, that's fashion right there. He's making a statement, "I'm cool, I'm relaxed, but I'm also edgy. You can't see my face, because there's a shyness in me but my soul is begging to …" Oh shit, did he just stab that old woman?'

Plans for Waterford Fashion Hour 2020 are already in place.

FESTIVALS

FYRE FESTIVAL STILL NOT AS BAD AS OXEGEN

VETERANS of the defunct Irish music festival Oxegen have openly laughed at the plight of festival-goers featured in Netflix's new controversial documentary of the Fyre Festival.

The festival, located in the Bahamas, is the subject of a documentary that details the fraudulent actions of the luxury festival's organisers, which left ticket-holders arriving to a field with a handful of tents, having paid thousands of dollars in admission and travel costs.

'Ha! Looks like a walk in the fucking park compared to Oxegen. What are they moaning about?' Netflix documentary watcher and former Oxegen ticket-holder Stephen

Geraghty scoffed while watching the events of Fyre Festival unfold.

While organisers of both festivals had similar issues with correctly spelling fairly basic words, this is where the similarities end, according to four-time Oxegen veteran Geraghty.

'These Fyre lads wouldn't have lasted a second in Oxegen. Now that was a proper shitshow,' Geraghty added, before recalling how the Kildare-based festival saw busloads of prisoners, on day release from Mountjoy Prison, ferried into Oxegen to engage in knife fights with festival goers in queues at burger vans.

The high rate of violence and skulduggery at Oxegen over the years was such that the majority of ticket-holders missed their favourite bands, due to requiring emergency surgery after their eyes were gouged out by scumbags.

High levels of scurvy were reported at the Irish festival, and medical

---

'These Fyre lads wouldn't have lasted a second in Oxegen. Now that was a proper shitshow'

---

professionals have traced the origins of an incurable strain of gonorrhoea to the 2009 edition of Oxegen. An estimated 47 tonnes of urine was unloaded onto the side of tents by hardcore Oxegen ticket holders, and several hundred died after getting stuck in mud.

'And don't get me started on the price of the fucking pints,' Geraghty concluded, after a woman in the Fyre documentary appeared on screen talking about how she had lost her life savings.

Suburban Dictionary

'Thanks; Penneys': A response to receiving a compliment on a garment likely made by a child in Bangladesh.

HEALTH

DID YOU DO THIS WHILE PREGNANT? YOUR CHILD IS PROBABLY FUCKED, SO

IN the latest study designed by think tanks with the express purpose of terrifying expectant mothers or parents of new-born babies, WWN can reveal that walking past butcher's shops between week 27 and week 29 of pregnancy can result in acute *childus fuckeduppa*, more commonly known as 'Your child is fucked, hen'.

Similar to studies that prove direct harm can befall you if you fail to do X or if you do too much Y, this new finding is vague enough to get expectant parents questioning whether they did in fact walk past a butcher's shop during that timeframe, and fails to provide any further details about whether or not the shop would have to have been open at the time. Despite this lack of information, it is incredibly specific about the consequences of having

done so, really upping the fear factor and ensuring a decent click-through rate for any site which hosts news of the report.

'New parents and pregnant women are always looking for reassurances that they're doing the best they can for their babies. This new report should give them a glimmer of fear that will prompt them to doubt and second-guess themselves for the next decade,' said Dr Wayne Vellarton, the world's leading medical clickbait compiler.

'We've sent our findings to pretty much every online magazine, and they'll all put their own little spin on it. You can look forward to seeing it pop up in your newsfeed over the next year, and we're certain it'll give you that little shiver of horror when you realise you may have adversely affected the health of your baby by

doing some random shit that you had never heard of. Because you could never

have heard of it. Because we just made it up.'

Keep an eye out for our upcoming guides, 'Five Things You Need to Know If You Walked Past a Butcher's Shop While Pregnant', and 'Walked Past a Butcher's Shop While Pregnant? Here's Five Things You Need to Know'.

Bill's Campaign Diary

Veteran journalist Bill Badbody takes a leave of absence from his day-to-day reporting at WWN HQ to pursue a career in politics, in the hope of securing a place as MEP in the European elections. This is his story.

Week 7

Delighted with my new campaign posters. There's nothing like that arousing feeling when you see yourself on the side of a bus. The remortgage will be totally worth it. Some snowflake complaints about my slogan 'Is Racism Really Racist?' Varadkar and his cronies are so scared of my political power they still haven't mentioned me once.

Disgusted to hear dozens of posters have been targeted by George Soros/EU-funded vandals. Biggest insult I read was calling me a right-wing Paudie Coffey. I'm way better looking, surely? No way I'm that fat and ugly. Must ask Anne how much Javier charges per session when they get back from their two-week exercise trip in Barbados.

On a Cork radio show debating against local MEP candidate, who, dare I say, didn't look one bit Irish. Foreign leftie loon wanted to scrap Direct Provision centres and give all the migrants free houses! Gave him a right piece of my mind. Started mumbling in pidgin English. Told him to go back to Nigeria and learn our language. He claimed then he was actually speaking Irish and was from Bantry. Total set-up by the EU. That tan was definitely fake, too, bordering on blackface, and no one called him racist?

Canvassing again and realised there needs to be a compulsory IQ test in order for these people to vote. Most of them I met today were under-educated and, dare I say, ignorant. No idea about chemtrails, 5G and hadn't even heard about the thousands of migrants coming here every day to claim the dole.

Reminded Fiachra about closing date for the elections again. Seems to have it all sorted. Although he looks a bit tired, God love him. Obviously thought it was just a 39-hour week. Lol. Now asking to be paid before the elections are over? Kids these days.

DISGUSTING! COUPLE EVICTED AFTER FAILING TO PAY MORTGAGE FOR 25 YEARS

A vulnerable couple who are mere years away from turning 100 years of age have been heartlessly evicted from their home after refusing, through no fault of their own, to meet a single repayment on the mortgage they took out 25 years ago.

Mary and Alan Higgenly, both 52, accidentally failed to repay a single cent of the £71,578 they borrowed from the bank when they took out a mortgage in June 1994, despite combined earnings of €200,000 today. However, they claim they wrote to the bank in 2011 in the ancient dead language of Biblical Hebrew but received no response after sending the letter via blind carrier pigeon.

'We've explored all options but the vipers that they are, the bank just want to destroy us. And for what? All for the £71,578 we never got around to paying back. God, some people are obsessed with money,' explained Mary Higgenly.

The Higgenlys, victims of a heinous plot by the bastard banks, are considering reporting their lender to the Hague for crimes against humanity.

'Banking tyrants such as this bank must be driven from the country, so honest people like Mary and Alan can retain the precious Irish soil that is theirs,' shared one member of a group called Sons of Éire, who turn up at evictions to support couples like Mary and Alan by shouting through a megaphone in between bouts of punching bank representatives in the face, while calling them violent fascists.

Asked had they considered availing of a free mortgage arrears support service like Abhaile, which has kept 95 per cent of people using personal insolvency arrangements in their homes, the couple instead drew WWN's attention to the €44 million GoFundMe campaign they have started, to help themselves remedy a situation not of their own making.

WWN Was There

𝔚aterford 𝔚hispers News

The unveiling of Irish Water, July 2013

What we said then: A supreme example of Enda Kenny's visionary leadership and his government's penchant for good, long-term planning. The rollout and setting up of this semi-state body should be the smoothest Ireland has ever seen. Bravo and congratulations to all involved. The modest fees incurred by the public shouldn't prove to be a problem either.

What we say now:
Hindsight is twenty-twenty, but all the Fine Gael spin doctors we interviewed at the time were full of praise for the project. To suggest there was any opposition or criticism at that exact time is simply not true. We're relieved to say that this was the last instance of poor delivery on public projects by Fine Gael.

DRINKING

CLAIM SLAB OF CANS WILL 'DO THE WHOLE CHRISTMAS' FOUND TO BE FRAUDULENT

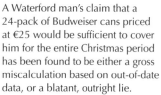

A Waterford man's claim that a 24-pack of Budweiser cans priced at €25 would be sufficient to cover him for the entire Christmas period has been found to be either a gross miscalculation based on out-of-date data, or a blatant, outright lie.

Mick Haskill made the claim while shopping with his wife Carrie in Waterford city centre at the weekend, after she had admonished him for putting the 12 litres of beer into the shopping trolley, smushing the bread and bananas.

Haskill countered his wife's 'Where are you going with that?' statement by stressing that it was nearly Christmas and they needed a stock of beer 'in case anyone came around to the house'. He assured Carrie that the purchase of a single slab would last until the Feast of the Epiphany – a claim that experts in Mick's drinking have balked at.

'Looking at the empirical data available to us, it is highly doubtful that this slab of cans is going to see December, let alone Christmas,' said a close drinking associate of Mr Haskill, in an exclusive interview with WWN.

'Twenty-four cans to last for thirty days? He'll have a quarter of that gone the first time *Die Hard* shows up on the telly. Rest assured, this isn't a slab for the season. This is the first of many, many slabs that will be downed over Advent. But sure when drink is that cheap, what are you going to do? Not get shitfaced every night? Come on now.'

Furthermore, it has been found that Carrie Haskill's claim that one tub of Roses would be sufficient for the entire Christmas period is also a 'crock of shite'.

MAN TOO HUNGRY TO CHANCE THE FALAFEL

A famished Waterford man currently trying to decide what to eat for lunch has confirmed he is actually 'too hungry' to try the falafel, but promised to make the decision to eat one someday, just not today.

Mark Ryan, 44, who could probably do with losing a few pounds now that he thinks about it, has instead opted for the lasagne and chips option on the menu, based on the fact that he knows exactly what it will taste like.

'Better the devil you know. If I buy that falafel thing for €6 and I don't like it, then that's a waste of money and I'll be starving by 3 o'clock,' Ryan debated with himself. 'Yeah, sure, I'll probably get the slump after this pasta and fried potato, but at least I won't be left hungry in work.'

Ryan later admitted to wanting to try the falafel, a mysterious food from a far-off land, for the past few years, knowing the patty made from ground chickpeas is a very popular lunch item for many health fanatics, due to its vegetarian content, but has just never gotten around to it yet.

'There's no meat in it and it's nearly 600 calories, so fuck that,' Ryan told himself again, desperately seeking solace. 'At least with the lasagne option, there's a spoonful of rocket and coleslaw that will cancel out all that salty, carby badness.'

VEGANISM

COMING OUT AS VEGAN TO YOUR BEEF-FARMING FATHER

AS veganism becomes a more prominent feature in news outlets seeking to draw their readers into pointless squabbling in their comment sections, WWN has decided it wants some of the action too.

We have taken it upon ourselves to provide would-be vegans still nestled in their ethically sourced, sustainable closets with a blueprint on how to come out to your father, who is an Irish beef farmer.

In order to truly help those of you wrestling with how best to tell your father that the screams and squeals of helpless animals being slaughtered really isn't your thing, we spoke to other vegans who came out to their beef-farming fathers.

Caoimhe Corrigan, 19, vegan

'He just died of a heart attack on the spot. The doctor said he'd never

seen anything like it. My da's heart literally exploded. It should have been medically impossible. The doctor was pretty fucked up after it all, to be honest. But I'm sure it'll be fine for you with your dad.'

David Neely, 36, vegan

'Yeah, his blood pressure's never been the same. He's on a year's supply of blood-pressure medication … but for every week. Mam says he's calmed down, but his face has remained this bright puce, red colour ever since I told him. There's the fact he hasn't actually spoken since I told him, too. He's a mute, and I came out as vegan about four years ago.'

Sarah Gobbin, 25, vegan

'I actually had a very positive response from my dad, all things considered. He waited until I left the house before he went insane, stripped down to nothing, ran around after the cows and literally bit into the hide of one of them. Poor thing.'

Gary Prentice, 21, vegan

'You know the joke "How do you know someone's a vegan? Don't

worry, they'll tell you". Well, not to be zero craic or anything, but it's actually hard to tell your beef-farming dad. He tried to understand, and amazingly he switched to dairy farming the next year. But then I explained about the not eating dairy products thing, 'cos that's still bad.

'He changed for me again, and I loved him even more for it. He shut down the farm, and just took up gardening as a profession, but when I told him about how plants have feelings and emotions too, and that he shouldn't mutilate grass with a lawnmower, he eventually told me to fuck off, which is fair enough.'

Deirdre Denning, 41, vegan

'We fell out immediately. I kept on at him to stop the slaughter but he's standing firm. At least he's let me work with the animals on making their lives as comfortable as possible until, ya know. The cows love the yoga classes and the chakra cleansing I do with them.'

Take heart in these examples of vegans sharing their life with their beef-farming fathers and take that brave step yourself today!

RADIO

HAVE YOUR PARENTS BEEN RADICALISED BY NEWSTALK? KNOW THE SIGNS

MORE and more people are reporting that their parents have been radicalised by Newstalk or, in even more worrying cases, by regional phone-in radio-show hosts.

Many children of parents have confirmed that when they discovered their parents were lurching towards near constant curmudgeonly complaints, a radio tuned to 106–108FM was within listening distance.

To stop this before it gets out of hand, learn to spot the signs.

- Are your parents saying 'This isn't what I pay my taxes for' at least 57 times a day?
- Do they fail to properly outline what exactly they do pay their taxes for?

- In your parents' eyes, is anyone under 30 anything other than a weed-smoking, hippy communist?
- Have they said 'This isn't what I pay my taxes for' again, and is it getting very fucking annoying?
- Do they believe political correctness has been sectioned under the Mental Health Act?
- Is the phrase 'Jaysus, give it a rest' or 'Here we go again' uttered when a female guest discusses anything about sexism, equal pay or women being bludgeoned to death by an angry mob?
- Have they expressed deep dissatisfaction with the government while also giving the impression that they'll break the sound barrier when it comes to running down to the local school to cast their vote for Fine Gael whenever an election is called?
- Do they say 'Now, I like him, he's good' whenever Ivan Yates is brought up in conversation?

If you are worried that this sounds like your parents, don't worry – help is available. Simply take a hammer to every radio in their home or cars, disconnect their Internet and burn all tabloid newspapers.

Suburban Dictionary

'A kip': A term used to describe taking a well-earned rest ... and Dublin.

114

TELEVISION

GRIM, GRITTY GRIMNESS: WE REVIEW RTÉ'S LATEST GRIM, GRITTY DRAMA

SUNDAY-night viewing on RTÉ has just changed for ever with the release of *Hell Streets*, the latest grim, gritty series from the state broadcaster, which presents a warts-and-all look at what is really going on in the crime-infested open sewers that we call the streets of our capital city.

Starring Íochra Ó Laoghaire-Wellington as tough Dublin detective Declan Hell, *Hell Streets* starts as it means to go on, with an opening scene that features a four-year-old girl injecting heroin into an infected vein while a flock of pigeons eats her recently overdosed mam on Grafton Street, with shoppers, probably culchies, just walking out of Brown Thomas without giving so much as a second glance.

Arriving on the scene of the grim death, Detective Hell – himself a borderline alcoholic after turning to the bottle in a bid to get over a cocaine addiction, which he had turned to to get over a crack cocaine addiction, which he had turned to to get over a troubled past where his dad hit him so hard he knocked him right onto the penis of the local paedophile priest – tasks himself with finding the source of the heroin that killed the woman, putting him in the line of fire of not just the local drug cartel, but the IRA, his crooked fellow cops, his old Bean an Tí from the one time he went to the Gaeltacht, and his bitch of an ex-wife.

Over the course of the 9.30–10.30 p.m. slot vacated by *Love/Hate*, *Hell Streets* takes an unflinching look at drugs, murder and heroin, but still finds time to include other subjects such as sex trafficking and forced prostitution – allowing for brief flashes of nipples on RTÉ, no less. This isn't the station of Our Lady any more. This isn't your grandmother's state broadcaster. This is a production starring some of South Dublin's best-connected acting talent doing northside accents to the best of their ability and wearing enough make-up to still look their *Tatler* best, but not so much that they don't look grim and gritty and, damn it, REAL.

All in all, *Hell Streets* is an unflinching, grim, gritty, warts-and-all, unwavering, grim, gritty, searing, dark, bleak, grim, gritty, down-and-dirty, true-to-life, grim, gritty griminygrits production full of cursing and partial nudity and scenes that viewers may find disturbing. It holds a mirror up to society and says, 'Look at yourselves, you cunts.' We recommend watching it, because it'll be all your co-workers talk about for the next eight weeks, so you may as well join in.

Community text alerts

There's no way the young one of the O'Riordans is 15 years old wearing that excuse of a skirt. Anything happens to her now and it's the poor lad's fault. The mother was the exact same.

BREAKING NEWS

'POLISH ANDY' UPGRADED TO JUST 'ANDY' BY CO-WORKERS AFTER EIGHT YEARS

MOVING scenes were recorded today in a Waterford warehouse, where workers officially announced their intention to henceforth refer to 'Polish Andy' as just 'Andy', honouring his eight years of tireless work at Mackin Supplies Ltd.

Andrzej Glik, 34, has politely endured constant references to 'Polish Andy' for eight years, despite the fact that no other Andy, Andrew or Andrzej has ever been on the books at Mackin Supplies, Ltd.

'It's just banter. Polish Andy … Eh, I mean Andy, is a dote and he loves it. It let's him know he's one of the gang,' downplayed manager Maggie Hanley.

Hanley refused to comment on rumours that the company would be in line for some sort of award for its trailblazing ways, but speculated out loud about whether or not the Nobel Prize Committee had a Best Manager award.

Speaking at the unveiling of his new name, Andrzej was visibly moved by the very forward-thinking and accepting gesture his colleagues took eight years to arrive at.

'It's actually pronounced like "Ann-Jay",' explained formerly 'Polish Andy', much to the confusion of his colleagues.

'Some people always have to be difficult,' muttered manager Hanley to herself, before instructing 'Polish Agata', who is from Lithuania, not to bother bringing out the cake celebrating Andy's eight years at the firm.

RYANAIR LAUNCH SEDATION KITS FOR CHILD PASSENGERS

BUDGET airline Ryanair is finally launching a range of sedation kits to subdue younger passengers in a bid to eradicate unwanted screaming, horseplay and general disruption during flights.

Welcomed by just about everybody who travels with the airline, the fast-acting kits will come at a cost of €100 for two-hour doses and €149.99 for five-hour doses, which will render annoying children unconscious, thus making way for a more peaceful, headache-free flight.

'About time, too,' one passenger boarding a flight from Dublin told WWN. 'There's nothing worse than noisy little shits whingeing all the way through your flight, or kicking the back of your seat in boredom.'

'The price isn't bad either when you split it between the rest of the passengers – fantastic idea!'

The new kits, which contain one syringe of benzodiazepines, will launch later this month, in time for the busy Christmas season and, depending on their success, they may also be rolled out for treating drunk or unruly passengers, too.

'If someone is going off on one during the flight, priority passengers will be allowed to buy a similar kit for adults, which of course will contain a much stronger dose,' a Ryanair spokesman stated.

Ryanair also confirmed that talkative passengers may also be administered the packs, depending on how chatty they are.

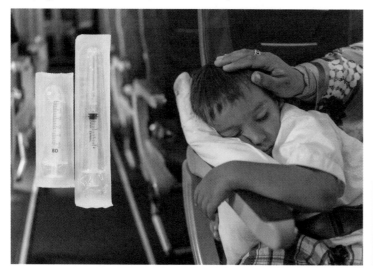

Animal facts

If the bee population continues to die out, young children's sex education will only ever extend as far as 'the birds'.

TRAVEL

'PRIORITY' PASSENGERS STILL QUEUING LIKE A PACK OF DOPES

A new report into 'priority' passengers using budget airlines has found that the large majority of them are still queuing like a pack of dopes, despite paying extra for their journeys.

With priority queues now almost double that of non-priority queues, the report found priority passengers are most likely to stand and wait for long periods if they pay for the service, while their non-paying counterparts sit patiently and wait for all of them to board.

'Sure, God love them. They've been standing there obediently for 40 minutes now,' scoffed non-priority passenger Martin Davis from the comfort of a seat at gate D7 departing for Rome.

'Who wants to sit on a plane longer than they should? I usually let everyone get on first, then get up, have a nice little stretch and then board the plane. Sure it's the same fecking seat I'll be sitting in, anyway. What's so priority about it?'

Suburban Dictionary

'He's getting too big for his boots': Refers to someone suffering from a rare form of gigantism, localised to the feet.

Charging up to €20 to queue in a parallel line, budget airline Ryanair has defended the system, stating that priority queues give their customers an air of self-importance and fill a psychological gap left there by their dreadful decision to fly with Ryanair.

'I suppose it makes a bad situation better for them,' explained a Ryanair spokesperson, 'kind of like when they used to put African Americans on the back of the bus. It made the white people feel better about themselves traveling on public transport.'

'I usually let everyone get on first, then get up, have a nice little stretch and then board the plane. Sure it's the same fecking seat I'll be sitting in, anyway. What's so priority about it?'

117

EQUALITY

IS THIS FAIR? THIS WOMAN GETS TREATED WELL BECAUSE SHE'S AN ABSOLUTE CRACKER

EQUALITY in the workplace is a hot-button issue that isn't going away anytime soon.

An ongoing, open dialogue is necessary and business leaders should never shy away from making the right decisions, which should see women afforded the same treatment, respect and opportunities that their male colleagues receive, irrespective of the industry.

It is important to highlight companies that are going about things the right way, despite receiving some criticism.

Take Naughton, Kelleher, Browne, O'Brien, Dowling, McCarthy,

> ### 'The way they sexualise her in her absence is degrading and frankly sickening'

O'Donovan and Associates as a commendable example. The all-male senior management team made sure to offer Susan Cleary special treatment in light of the historic barriers once put in the way of women in the workplace.

Cleary, an absolute cracker by all accounts, has garnered special attention, comments and offers from her male superiors and peers, proving that equality is closer than we think. However, as is often the

case when bravely making history, the management has been criticised by some negative naysayers.

'I don't think I'm wrong in stating Susan looks uncomfortable in their presence, and while they always acquiesce to her requests for a half-day for this, that and the other, the way they sexualise her in her absence is degrading and frankly sickening,' remarked one female co-worker, who'll get nowhere with a petty, jealous attitude like that.

The modern men's inclusive and equality-driven mindset extends to Cleary outside the office as well, with polite, courteous and self-described 'male feminists' always pretending to carefully listen to her opinions, approach her at bars to 'just chat', open doors for her and generally ignore all other women once they clap eyes on her.

'Something tells me Cleary is more equal in the eyes of men than I am,' snarled one battleaxe who would want to take a long, hard look at herself, learn to smile a little, and stop being so jealous of Cleary, her legs and her body, which are unreal in fairness.

Fullmindness

Make gratitude part of your routine by thanking the people you hate for their ongoing stupidity.

HUNTING

MEET THE IRISH HUNT WHO SWAPPED FOXES FOR PAEDOPHILES

UP until the last ten years, paedophile hunting was a relatively unknown practice in Ireland, despite the apparent large number of paedophiles living here. However, with the emergence of social-networking sites, the phenomenon has gone from strength to strength, with it now becoming one of the nation's favourite pastimes.

WWN travelled to County Tipperary this week to visit a local fox hunt that has decided to take matters into their own hands, and swap hunting foxes for paedophiles.

'We're basically killing two birds with the one stone here,' explained master of hounds Thomas Kinsella. 'Hunting innocent animals has had its day in Ireland, but we still enjoy the social aspect of the hunt and began discussing what could replace the fox. The obvious answer was paedophiles and sex offenders.'

In May last year, the Tipperary horse enthusiasts launched their first-ever

> **'There's nothing more enjoyable than hearing one of them squeal for their life while being ripped to shreds by the dogs'**

paedophile hunt outside the town of Fethard, with the pilot day attracting thousands of riders.

'Many of the people brought weapons like maces and swords, which wasn't the plan,' Kinsella said. 'We wanted to keep it traditional and let the hounds do all the chasing down and killing. Besides, killing them with weapons is way too quick a death for these sick bastards. There's nothing more enjoyable than hearing

one of them squeal for their life while being ripped to shreds by the dogs. Nothing!'

It is estimated that one in every ten people in rural Ireland are raging paedophiles, with the hunt now claiming to take out five to ten per day.

'Instead of a horn, I use an electronic speaker that blares out ice-cream truck music to bring them out. It's like shooting fish in a barrel really, but it's great fun all the same. Once dead, or nearly dead, we then scalp them as a trophy – because obviously humans don't have tails.'

However, the paedophile hunt has come under fire after brutally savaging an innocent man who was just out walking with his dogs last September.

'Look, we're bound to have some teething problems, and that man was wearing socks with sandals, but all in all we're slowly eradicating child abusers from the general population,' Kinsella finished.

Animal facts

Giraffes were first created in 1876, after scientists successfully crossed a horse with a cheetah.

RELATIONSHIPS

NEW TINDER SETTING MAKES SURE CULCHIES DON'T RIDE THEIR COUSINS

POPULAR dating app Tinder has released an update featuring several new revisions aimed at the rural-Ireland dating scene, such as an increased search radius which allows people to find mates who are up

> **'The rural-Ireland dating scene has been plagued for years by incidents where perfect strangers pair up together, only to realise down the line that they're third cousins'**

for the ride, even if they live in the arsehole of nowhere, while also checking to make sure mates don't copulate within their own bloodlines.

Other features include checkboxes for the amount of road frontage a potential match might have, allowing people to not waste their time on someone who doesn't even have any land, and a new system that will eliminate anyone who has notions about themselves – all of which will make Tinder the number-one matchmaking tool in the country, according to bosses at the firm.

'The rural-Ireland dating scene has been plagued for years by incidents where perfect strangers pair up together, only to realise down the line that they're third cousins,' said Martin

Tinder, owner of Tinder Worldwide, the conglomerate over Tinder Enterprises.

'Our new facial recognition software will give people a "Slow down there, chief" notification if a guy matches with his mother's cousin's daughter, or the like.

'"Are they Protestants?", "Do they not drink tea?" … Loads of new features that will make sure country folk get a match. This does narrow down the amount of potential riding that culchies will be able to do, but we're sure it's what they want.'

So far, nobody in rural Ireland has downloaded the update.

Fullmindness

It's important to be present in the moment. The clearer the mind, the more room there is to focus on that one time in first year you wet your pants.

SOCIAL MEDIA

NEWS ARTICLES ON 'CHILD SUICIDE GAME' TARGETING VULNERABLE PARENTS

VULNERABLE parents are in danger from clickbait-style news articles designed to spread fear and panic around a self-harming game called 'Momo', WWN can confirm.

Experts have warned children that the majority of the news articles depict an image of a distorted woman with sensational headlines, and can lure their parents into a state of panic in a matter of seconds.

'If you see your parents reading such articles, please reassure them that everything is going to be okay,' said Thomas Jockey, chief executive of WebSafe Ireland. 'Parents may go temporarily insane and start searching through your devices. There may also be a period of time when your YouTube app will be deleted in exchange for the YouTube Kids app, but don't worry – this is only temporary.'

The articles – which have now gone more viral than the game they were covering, thus exposing millions of children to something they had never heard of before – feature across all mainstream media platforms, are more or less all worded in the same scaremongering style, and come with thousands of naïve comments from parents.

'I caught my mother searching through my iPad and had to have "the talk" with her,' explained seven-year-old Saoirse Hogan from Lucan. 'Once you explain that you're not so stupid to go harm yourself over a stupid game, they seem to calm down a bit.' Before adding, 'Sure God bless their cotton socks, if they only knew the real stuff we watch online, they'd actually have reason to be scared.'

Bill's Campaign Diary

Veteran journalist Bill Badbody takes a leave of absence from his day-to-day reporting at WWN HQ to pursue a career in politics, in the hope of securing a place as MEP in the European elections. This is his story.

Week 8

Two weeks to go and the mainstream, left-wing, corrupt, cultural-Marxist media are refusing to have me on to debate the total destruction of Ireland. Waited in the RTÉ car park for David McCullagh after a *Prime Time* debate. Started shouting 'Get off me!' like a little wimp. Forced him to ask me the exact same debate questions, but he managed to get out of the headlock. Hope it took him ages to change those tyres.

Apologised online for slashing David McCullagh's tyres and assaulting him. I'll admit it wasn't in the best taste, or my finest moment, but he drove me to it. Perhaps also wrong of me to say 'Why doesn't *Prime Time* investigate THIS?', while grabbing my crotch. Media, of course, making a bigger deal out of it than it was. Poor Ben Gilroy is losing his mind now too in frustration, hitting walls with hurleys. They're making us all look crazy now. Gemma too.

Anne's phone going to voicemail today. Seeing nothing but pictures of her beside the beach. I suppose swimming is a big part of getting fit, but surely those cocktails are fattening? But look, I'm not the personal trainer or nutritionist. I'm sure Javier is keeping a close eye on her calorie intake over there.

Fiachra informs me we only made €11.50 from campaign donations, which proves my point that we're being shadow banned by Facebook and Google, hiding our donation posts. Was really counting on that to pay him.

Revenue sending me threatening letters now for unpaid taxes, despite me telling them I'm not paying VAT any more. Returned to sender saying, 'Stop wasting our money and I'll pay.' Besides, I'll be living in Europe soon anyway, so best of luck getting that.

WWN Was There

Waterford Whispers News

Marriage Equality Referendum, May 2015

What we said then: The Irish public was asked whether it wanted to allow man to marry man, woman to marry woman, creepy uncle to marry pet dog, and in its infinite lack of wisdom it said 'Yes'.

Seek confession, apologise to your priest. Look up 'how to perform a self-exorcism' tutorial on YouTube. And, while you're at it, why don't you tell me what I'm supposed to tell my kids, huh? How am I supposed to explain to them why their father is so consumed and blinded by hate that he dragged them out to gay pride with a 'you're all going to hell' poster? And for what? A 'Yes' vote to win anyway?

What we say now: A rare foray into opinion pieces for my good self. I was in a dark place then and am deeply ashamed of my behaviour. Those who criticise me may say I am only sorry because of those pictures that were circulated online of my friend Jorge performing the Heimlich manoeuvre on me while we were both naked, but it has nothing to do with that. I simply evolved as a person and came to accept myself and marriage equality.

INVESTIGATION LAUNCHED TO FIND OUT WHERE REST OF MEN'S TROUSERS HAVE GONE

FASHION police have launched an official investigation into the disappearance of the final few inches of men's trousers, a full two years after members of the public first brought the troubling occurrence to the attention of authorities.

Accused of ignoring reports made by the public, the police investigation has been dismissed by many concerned citizens as too little, too late.

'And when we find out where they've gone, then what? Have a look around, it's a fuckin' epidemic,' explained 36-year-old Niall Tierney, who is increasingly scared by the fashion choices made by men younger than himself. 'I brought this to their attention years ago, seriously, and I was dismissed like I was crazy. Now it's affected all trousers everywhere.'

Speaking at a press conference which formally announced the investigation, lead detective for the FP, Paul Neary, outlined the problem.

'Bare ankles, no socks, we've even heard reports of people being able to see the beginnings of calf muscles on some trouser-wearing men. We know people out there are scared, but believe me when I say we will get to the bottom of this,' Neary said, going on to state that the culprits responsible for this phenomenon will be brought to justice.

Some men affected are reportedly unaware they are victims at all, stating that their trousers have always been missing the last several inches and that it is fine.

'Sadly, we are too late to help some people. There's talk of therapy and support groups, but it's just too late in these cases,' Neary explained before breaking down in tears.

Suburban Dictionary

'Eejit': A respected and revered member of society, known for their smarts and nobility.

RELATIONSHIPS

IS JAMES SUDDENLY ATTRACTIVE NOW THAT HE HAS A GIRLFRIEND? WE INVESTIGATE

REPORTS coming into WWN's sister publication, *Gash*, are speculating on the relative attractiveness of James, now that another woman has deemed him worth the effort and has begun a relationship with him.

The phenomenon of men previously discounted suddenly becoming attractive when someone else takes an interest has been debated for decades, but James's recent acquirement of a partner who clearly sees something in him or sure why would she bother could well be the most demonstrable example yet.

'His stubble is just the right amount. Like, it used to veer into the "I'm just not arsed shaving" length but it's always just the right shape now. Fuck, how did I not see this before?' confirmed one woman previously not into James but now sort of considering it.

A brief review of old photos James posted on his social media accounts confirms the theory that 'Shit, wait, was he sort of a ride all along? A secret ride, a ride in plain sight.'

While some accounts of James's level of attractiveness are conflicting, there is no doubt that he has been dressing much better recently, but that was hardly his idea now, was it?

'He's actually quite broad-shouldered now that I look at him. It's those tighter-fitting shirts he's wearing. They're not super tight, but just tight enough, ya know. Hmmm,' confirmed another woman who sort of, could have, had a thing with James at one point about a year ago but it never really happened and now she's regretting it because, 'I mean, Jesus, have you been on Tinder lately? The absolute state of it.'

James's Instagram activity has increased tenfold since gaining a girlfriend, with a variety of photos and stories being posted showcasing that he likes to eat brunch, drink the occasional glass of red wine, and do outdoor activities.

'Fuck, I didn't have him down as the do-things, drink-wine, eat-brunch kinda guy, but that's all I was looking for,' cursed another woman who runs into James now and again on nights out because of a mutual friend but she just wasn't in the right frame of mind to pursue a relationship.

While James's girlfriend hasn't yet issued an official 'Hands off' warning in the form of a cryptic, inspirational-quote meme about knowing when you have a good thing, experts speculate that she's noted the increase in people commenting on and liking his photos.

Conclusion: We fucked up. Just look at him. How did we not see it before?

Animal facts

'Jumpy Green Yoke' was briefly considered as a possible name for what we now refer to as a frog.

EXCLUSIVE

WE TALK EXCLUSIVELY TO FAMILY WHO REFUSE TO GET VACCINATIONS

IN response to the growing trend of parents choosing to forego vaccinating their children, which they claim causes autism, the WWN Investigates team reached out to a number of 'concerned parents' in a bid to give a voice to those shunned by the complicit mainstream media, who are in the pockets of the Big Pharma and Normal-Sized Pharma companies.

Keen to offer a platform denied to them by large media organisations that want to keep the truth about vaccines suppressed, WWN met with the Bresmond family, who made the decision not to vaccinate their three young children because they wanted to bring them up free from the brain-controlling chemicals placed in vaccines by a shadowy network of people who they wouldn't outright say were Jewish, but reading between

the lines, we're pretty confident the Bresmonds think they control everything.

Frustratingly north of monosyllabic, the Bresmond parents, John and Catherine, seemed reluctant to talk as we knelt down on the freshly turned soil in Glasnevin Cemetery and hit record on our Dictaphone.

Questions about the benefits of not getting the HPV vaccine were stubbornly ignored, while follow-up queries about why guarding their children against meningitis, measles, mumps, rubella, diphtheria, tetanus, whooping cough and polio, among other diseases, was just 'brainwashing propaganda' went unanswered.

We couldn't put our fingers on why they were so reluctant to speak out. Perhaps they feared they were being watched. They didn't say who

was watching them but, going out on a limb, we'd reluctantly suggest they were once again referring to Jews.

According to the etching on their tombstones, John and Catherine are both 35, and while WWN is not being critical of them – maybe they're deaf or simply had a cough and lost their voices – it would have been a nice courtesy to inform us in advance so we could hire an ASL interpreter or postpone the interview for another time.

Similarly Jack, 8, Ellie, 7, and One World Order Look It Up People!!!, 4, were all equally silent.

We can only conclude that anti-vaccine campaigners can't say they are being silenced by the media and then, when we arrive to interview them, refuse to talk with us, too.

Community text alerts

Short notice, but jury-duty volunteers needed in district court as the accused killed the last 12 jurors.

RELATIONSHIPS

'RIDE EVERYTHING WITH A PULSE!': THE TOUCHING LAST WORDS OF IRISH GRANDMOTHER

FIDELMA Hickey, a 91-year-old Waterford woman, sadly passed away on Wednesday, but not before imparting some inspirational words to her three granddaughters who were at her bedside during her final moments. Words that have since gone viral and featured in the pages of *The New York Times*, *The Sydney Morning Herald*, LadBible and *The Daily Telegraph*, among thousands of other print and online publications.

'Granny suffered no fools, that's for sure,' youngest granddaughter Alva, 25, shared with WWN. 'She was a trailblazer, a modern woman who grew up in a not-so-modern time, and her final words will stay with me for ever.'

Hickey, a devoted grandmother, sought to pass on some words of wisdom in her final breaths, and her words have astounded and inspired those who have heard her story as it was shared online.

'I don't care if it's a woman or a man or whatever they call themselves that you're shacking up with, just shag them seven ways 'til Sunday,'

Hickey can be heard telling her granddaughters, clearly struggling for oxygen, on audio privately recorded by her family.

'If they have a small one, a long, fat one or a bendy one. Or, ya know, if it's a she – the longer and wider the tongue the better. Take it from me. Just promise me you'll jump up on whatever it is and get your kicks, love. Ride everything with a pulse!' the inspirational 91-year-old said, now coughing through the pain.

'I remember one fella and I said "Oh, that'll never fit in here." Jesus, sure aren't I haunted at least once a week by the thought of never giving it a go.

'My one regret in life is that I can count on only one hand the times I had an orgy. Girls, if I could do it all again, I'd have dumped your grandfather in a heartbeat and turned riding young fellas into an Olympic sport,' Hickey said in her poignant final breath.

The cries of anguish and loss from her 92-year-old husband Noel Hickey could also be clearly heard.

What a woman. What advice!

BREAKING THAT CHOCOLATE WAS SUPPOSED TO LAST WOMAN THE WEEK!

DESPITE her best-laid plans, executed to near perfection by one local Sligo woman, the modest supply of chocolate purchased as part of the 'big shop' on Sunday evening, and meant to last until the following Sunday, has not made it past Tuesday night, WWN can exclusively reveal.

Lorna Govan, 31, had placed a large Dairy Milk Oreo bar in the top press in her kitchen alongside a Twix, a packet of Maltesers and a Freddo caramel bar, and had every intention of dipping into her supply across six evenings.

However, come Tuesday evening, her plan lay in tatters.

'Ah, what am I like?' Govan sighed, really disappointed in herself, it has to be said.

While Govan was kicking herself for her lack of self-control, research shows that not a single person has perfected the art of spacing out chocolate consumption when it's bought in bulk.

'Buying in one big go for the weeks and months ahead never works,' confirmed chocolate consumption scientist Dr Neville Heggary. 'Several separate trips to the shops, over the course of the week, is still the best method if you're hoping to avoid that sense of "Bollocks, I wasn't supposed to eat this much."'

The real tragedy emerging from the chocolate chow-down is that it's only Tuesday, and Lorna has four evenings in front of the TV without chocolate at her disposal.

EXCLUSIVE INTERVIEW

INTERVIEWING Carl Hughes isn't easy, but after months of discussions with the Department of Justice and senior garda figures, WWN was allowed access to the unrepentant psychopath.

Hughes might not be the only psychopath walking among the Irish population, but he is the most notorious.

'D'you expect me to apologise or something?' Hughes sneered from behind some bulletproof plexiglass, housed in a straitjacket for his own safety and flanked by 12 security guards.

'I LIKE TO LEAVE THE EMPTY MILK CARTON IN THE FRIDGE'

'Sure, I like to leave the empty milk carton in the fridge. And given a chance, I'd do it in your fridge too,' sicko Hughes said, clearly deeply disturbed.

Hughes was once a fully functioning member of civil society and even shared a flat with three friends in Cork city. Like a lot of housemates, Hughes and his friends pooled their money to purchase toiletries and basics like bread and milk.

Hughes' psychopathy emerged when the communal milk carton would approach empty. Instead of using up the last dribbles of milk and putting it in the bin, the madman placed the empty carton back in the fridge for his housemates to discover, leaving them bereft and milkless.

'Boo-fucking-hoo, I get my kicks where I can, and I am not apologising for it. Did I think "Carl, man, just put the milk in the recycling bin after washing it out a bit?" Of course, but fuck me, that's a lot of effort,' Hughes said, clearly guilt-free about the crimes he has perpetrated.

The victims Hughes left behind still carry the scars to this day.

'It's simple, you just put it in the bin and say "Lads, next one in the shops, can ye grab a pint of milk?" but Carl just let us go on thinking that a milk carton had some milk in it,' explained housemate and key witness at Hughes' trial, Michael Norton.

'I'd do it time and time again. I'd reach for the milk, preparing my hand, arm and shoulder socket for a substantial, milky weight but I'd lift up an empty carton. It's sick. He's sick. How dare he. It's the ultimate betrayal. I'd like to see the death penalty brought back just for him.'

If you know of anyone who knowingly leaves an empty milk carton in the fridge, contact the gardaí immediately.

Health and fitness tip

Scraping the white top off a pint of Guinness will halve its calorie count. But don't throw it away, it makes for a great moisturiser or sexual lubricant.

RELATIONSHIPS

HOUSEMATES NOT AS QUIET AT RIDING AS THEY THINK

DO you enjoy bringing your partner back to your flat for a quickie, safe in the knowledge that your copulation is quiet enough to go unnoticed by your housemates? Well, you're in for a surprise, after a poll among apartment- and house-dwellers showed that almost all riding done in a shared living environment is almost 100 per cent audible to all people within.

Of the 100,000 people polled, 99,999 of them confirmed that the gyrations and grunts of their flatmates were loud enough to be heard through several walls, with the remaining one person admitting to being deaf since birth.

This came as a complete surprise to flatmates around the country, who could have sworn that they were being 'as quiet as a gentle breeze' during bouts of either riding someone

> **'Using sensitive listening equipment, we can easily detect the sounds of Derek upstairs fingering some young one he brought home'**

rotten or getting rode rotten, while their housemate was in the next room.

'Using sensitive listening equipment, we can easily detect the sounds of Derek upstairs fingering some young one he brought home from Coppers,' said a spokesperson for the study, wearing earplugs to drown out the terrible mating sounds of a drunk Carlow man.

'Truly, nobody is ever as quiet as they think they are during love-making. This may come as distressing news to anyone still living with their parents who brings a girlfriend or boyfriend home, who may have been under the impression that their folks didn't know there was a bit of riding going on. They knew, they absolutely knew.'

Although the news comes as a surprise to them, most flat-sharing stranger-bangers have stated that this is 'as quiet as they're likely to be this side of the grave'.

Community text alerts

Four lads in a white Hiace van driving into housing estates, looking into people's driveways. Called Peter Casey.

BREAKING NEWS

VICTOR'S SECRET LAUNCH SEXY LINGERIE FOR MEN

ADDRESSING a much-needed vacuum in the Irish men's lingerie market, American menswear giant Victor's Secret has announced it is opening its first Irish store early next year.

The alluring brand, which is a byword for classy, understated male elegance in the boudoir, is sure to find popularity in Ireland.

'Delicately stitched, crotchless boxers; chiffon Y-fronts; lace PJs – we've got it all,' announced Victor Lynskey at a press conference announcing the brand's arrival in Ireland.

Set up in response to the boring, ugly and visionless boxer-brief brands men were left with as their underwear of choice, Victor's Secret now accounts for 78 per cent of all men's lingerie sales worldwide, and their Irish launch has captured the imagination of men around the country.

'I like the see-through ones. You know the patterned ones with the plunging V-line that shows off your mickey? I used to order them online, but having a shop here will be handier,' shared Dublin man Paul Keneally.

'I wear them just for me. I'll be honest, I get a bit of a kick out of it when I'm at work and the only one who knows I'm wearing assless, lace cut-outs and nipple tassels underneath my overalls,' added Paul.

Victor's Secret's flagship 2,000 sq. ft store opens on Henry Street in February, just in time for Valentine's Day.

HOUSING

THREE OTHER WAYS TO TORTURE YOURSELF AFTER SEARCHING FOR ACCOMMODATION IN DUBLIN

DO you have a perverse desire to heap pain and suffering upon yourself? Have you already gone down the route of searching for accommodation in Dublin, seeking out an acceptable room, house or apartment for a monthly rent less than the entire GDP of a small Caribbean island?

Don't worry, the torturous search is never a short and easy one, so you can continue to fulfil your masochistic needs for some time to come.

However, if you eventually grow tired of that never-ending parade of pain, indignity and shame, there are other torture options which, if not as painful, are close enough.

1. Washing your eyeballs out with broken glass that's been soaked in vinegar

Hmm, yeah, that'll do it. Okay, the screams aren't as haunting as when you're being shown around a pokey one-bed apartment which is going for €1,800 a month, but we're not torture miracle workers.

2. Attaching a barbed-wire cable to your nipples, hooking the other end up to Lewis Hamilton's F1 Mercedes and letting him thump down on the accelerator

The speed of the F1 vehicle will mean that your nipples will be torn clean off, but the pain will be short-lived, so not in the same league as the drawn-out nature of being number 47 in a queue for a house viewing with a laundry list of Celtic-Tiger-era structural defaults.

3. Chopping off limbs with a blunt saw operated by someone with arthritis

The agony endured would see you drift in and out of consciousness and yet still isn't strictly comparable to the pain of paying rent that is double the cost of the mortgage for the owner, for one of the three rooms in their cramped, energy-inefficient hovel.

TRIPPING KIDS AS THEY RUN AROUND RESTAURANTS TO BE MADE LEGAL

LONG-AWAITED legislation is about to be passed that will allow fully grown adults to trip kids running around their feet in restaurants, pubs, trains, wedding receptions, and all public areas across the country.

Until now, spirited youngsters were legally entitled to run as fast as they fucking could, wherever they liked, despite the immediate proximity of dangerous kitchen implements and glassware, or even adults just trying to relax and have a few pints.

From Monday, adults will be able to trip up kids with no legal recourse, whether they do it by simply sticking out their foot at the right time, or pushing out a stool in front of them just as they fly past.

'The law we had was madness. Kids were allowed to tear around restaurants, and adults weren't allowed to floor them. Insane,' said Judge Anne Barry, prepping herself for some serious tripping in the coming weeks.

'It was actually a crime. You could get arrested for assault on a minor. Thankfully, we as a nation have finally gotten some sense. Maybe now kids will think twice before they start turning a coffee shop into a decathlon, or a cinema into Mondello Park.'

The legislation also permits stopping kids on wheeled modes of transport by pushing a stick into the spokes of a passing BMX, or just clotheslining some cocky teenager from his passing skateboard.

HOUSING

RENTER NOT GOING TO RISK ASKING LANDLORD TO FIX ANYTHING

ALTHOUGH there are several things that 'need doing' in their one-bedroom Phibsborough apartment, renters Ian Gurnin and his girlfriend Hannah Lennon have decided to either ignore them or hire a handyman out of their own pocket to avoid pissing off their landlord about anything.

'You can see a right bit of mould in the shower there because the fan is fucked, but I'm saying nothing,' said Gurnin, who doesn't want to risk a hike in his €1,600-a-month rent.

'I'll get one in PowerCity and tackle it myself at the weekend. Sure how hard can it be? I'm not an electrician but I'll take my chances with wires in a bathroom quicker than I'll ask himself to send around a tradesman. That's deposit go-bye-bye, and that'd be the absolute best-case scenario.'

Like most renters in Ireland, Ian and Hannah know they can be replaced by a higher-paying tenant at the drop of a hat and, as such, are more than happy to live in sub-standard accommodation without 'causing any fuss'.

'Yeah, there's a big nail sticking out of the wall, but I really only catch myself on it about twice or three times a day,' said Hannah, heading to the doctor's to get a tetanus shot.

'It's just great to have a place that's only an hour's commute from work, and really cheap, too. What more could we ask for? Oh yeah, an oven that works and hot water and a toilet that flushes properly, and any number of other jobs … But look, they add to the charm of the place, don't they?'

UPDATE: Gurnin and Lennon have been evicted by their landlord, who could psychically sense they were thinking bad things about him.

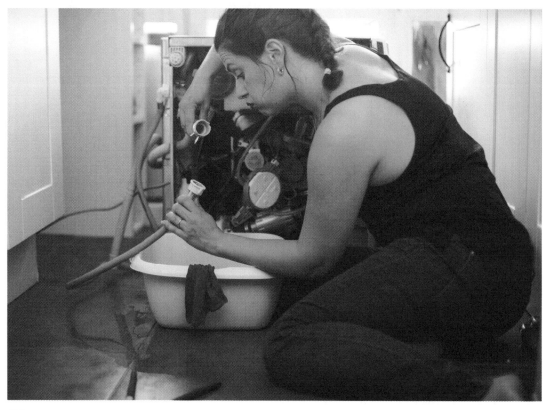

DINING

RESTAURANT CUSTOMERS TO BE FORCED TO PRINT DIETARY NEEDS ON FOREHEADS

DIETARY needs such as gluten intolerance and nut allergies will have to be permanently imprinted on customer's foreheads, according to new proposals laid out by the government today.

Minister for Health Simon Harris is reportedly aiming to introduce the new measures from 1 September this year in a bid to cut down on the number of 'annoying pricks' returning dishes to the kitchen because they didn't read the allergen warnings properly.

The announcement will force coeliacs and people with food intolerances to tattoo their dietary needs right onto their foreheads, to warn waiting staff about what type of person they're dealing with. The

> **'Yes, there will be a lot of people with tattoos on their heads, but at least they'll be alive and not choking to death'**

move is expected to save thousands of tonnes of wasted food every year, and probably some lives.

'It doesn't have to be too big,' Simon Harris insisted today while detailing the new proposal backed by the Food Safety Authority of Ireland. 'All they need to do is get a small tattoo anywhere on their forehead,

so that everyone knows what kind of intolerance the person has.'

The proposal will also force vegans to be branded, as well as people with shellfish and dairy intolerances, and people with religious requirements such as halal.

'Yes, there will be a lot of people with tattoos on their heads, but at least they'll be alive and not choking to death or being struck down by whatever God they're trying to please,' Minister Harris finished.

Health and fitness tip

When carb-loading, be sure to keep your back straight, engage your core and lift from your legs.

WATERFORD WOMAN CONTRACTS CONJUNCTIVITIS IN HER THIRD EYE

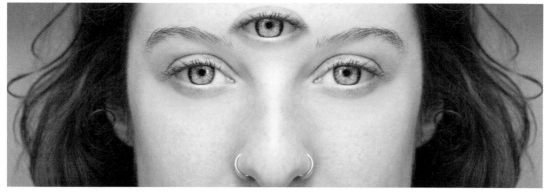

A County Waterford woman has become the first-known human in history to contract pink eye in her third eye, and is currently being treated with new, experimental therapy in Dublin, WWN has learned.

Fullmindness

'Fullmindness' in the workplace is important and companies have never been more serious about staging a yoga workshop instead of increasing pay for employees and reducing workload and stress.

Alison Cooley first noticed the condition late last year during a group meditation session when she felt the overwhelming urge to scratch a deep-set irritation in the middle of her brain.

Following four weeks of unbearable itching that she could not alleviate, the 34-year-old underwent several MRI and sonar scans to source the route of the problem, only for doctors to find a slight swelling and pink discoloration on her pineal gland.

'Not being able to scratch my third eye was agony,' the woke daughter-of-two recalled. 'I noticed my vibrations were off, too, and my chakras were all over the place, so when I found out it was only a viral infection in my third eye, I was somewhat relieved.'

Ms Cooley's third eye has since cleared up after surgeons performed keyhole brain surgery, carefully navigating through her head and rubbing anti-bacterial cream onto the surface of her third eye. However, two more people from her yoga class have since contracted the infection.

'Pink eye is very contagious, and we believe the other patients must have contracted it while meditating with Ms Cooley as all their vibrations harmonised together,' a doctor concluded.

THE COMPLETE LIST OF CHEESES THAT ARE BETTER THAN HAVING A BOYFRIEND

WHETHER you are currently single, dating, or in a long-term relationship, time and time again the question that gnaws at people is: 'But would I just be happier if I started seeing cheese romantically and consuming it full time?'

Gash, Ireland's leading publication aimed at women and womanly women stuff, has picked the brains of the country's leading cheesemongers, who have recommended a number of cheeses that provide more joy, support,

positive reinforcement and general benefits than a boyfriend.

Brie
Won't go on a rant about football any time soon. Delicious.

Feta
Thus far, feta has never cheated on you, and is infinitely better than having an argument with your boyfriend in an underground car park when he says, 'I can't remember where I parked the car.'

Gouda
Better than sex. A simple fact backed up by science.

Every other cheese
Nervous men reading this information will obviously be a little devastated but, honestly, some of these cheeses don't smell as bad as you and certainly last longer.

TRADESMAN WILL GLADLY DO A FEW OTHER JOBS FOR FREE WHILE HE'S THERE

WATERFORD plumber Liam Rollins may have bills to pay, he may have a schedule to keep, and he may have several other customers waiting for him to arrive, but his current client just asked him to bleed her radiators while he's there, and there's not really much chance he's going to pass up an opportunity like that.

> **'And as for asking for payment? Sure, isn't she paying me for the first job. Why would I want money for the second one?'**

Currently in Sheila O'Harris's house doing a siphon change on her upstairs bathroom toilet, as scheduled and agreed upon, Rollins had intended to get the fairly quick and hassle-free job done and dusted in time to head to his other appointments, in order to do their jobs in exchange for money.

However, these plans were scuppered by Ms O'Harris, who asked him if he'd 'bleed them radiators while you're there, it won't take you long', thus triggering the legally binding slave-labour contract that all tradespeople must abide by in Ireland.

'Bleeding and balancing a heating system is about an hour's work and I normally charge about €50 for it, but seeing as I was on the premises when she asked me, I'm kinda fucked,' sighed Rollins, in anticipation of all his other customers giving him a bollocking for the rest of the day.

'By law, when a tradesman gets asked to do a job while at another job, he can't turn around and say "Actually, no, I've got a load of shit to do and you should have asked me in advance." You just have to do it. And as for asking for payment? Sure, isn't she paying me for the first job. Why would I want money for the second one? What am I, a man with a family to feed? Come on now!'

UPDATE: Ms O'Neill was not happy with the way Rollins did the free work around her house and has told her friends to avoid him if they need anything done.

Community text alerts

Apologies for last week's alert, when we said the new people in Mary Street were Syrian. They're actually Pakistani, and doctors ... not terrorists. Sorry again.

MOTORING

WOMEN CALL FOR BIGGER MAKE-UP MIRROR ON CAR WINDSCREEN

FEMALE humans worldwide have called on car manufacturers to increase the size of the 'make-up mirror', located at the centre of the windscreen, claiming that the design does not reflect the whole face and is practically useless for women.

'Obviously, whatever eejit designed this was a man who had zero experience in applying make-up,' voiced motorist Donna Carey, who has begun an online petition to correct the mirror dimensions.

'Even though I have the mirror facing directly at me all the time, I can only see my eyes and have to either adjust the mirror and sometimes my own head in order to get my

Fullmindness

Sleeping in bed all day is a great way to distract your mind from your horrible existence. It prevents you from dragging everyone else down with your manic depression. Stay there for days, if you must. Months, even.

lipstick on. This, of course, is highly dangerous, as it distracts from my driving and something needs to be done about that.'

Pointing to a male-dominated manufacturing industry as the problem, women drivers behind the campaign urged male designers to take their products more seriously when developing them, and to put more thought and consideration into producing female-orientated items.

'It's not rocket science,' implied another campaigner. 'And fair enough, they did manage to include a handy button which lowers the mirror slightly

> **'Obviously, whatever eejit designed this was a man who had zero experience in applying make-up'**

when needed, but why not just make the height bigger? It doesn't make any sense whatsoever.

'Men are complete idiots, sometimes. God love them.'

SPORT

AMERICAN FOOTBALL

LOCAL MAN WILL NEVER BE AMERICAN, NO MATTER HOW MUCH HE TALKS ABOUT THE NFL

'I genuinely think he's of the belief that the more he talks about it, the less real the fact he's from Ardkeen will feel'

AN overexcited local Waterford man is still unpacking all the events from last weekend's NFL action, seemingly unaware of the fact that no matter how much he talks about the sport, it will not magically grant him US citizenship.

Niall Cossan was mulling over the latest round of games during his lunch break today, reserving most of his NFL chat for the Seahawks' victory over the Cardinals.

'Honestly, no one cares,' Cossan was told in no uncertain terms by a co-worker who insisted the 23-year-old's NFL obsession may hint at a larger problem.

'It's sad to watch, actually,' confirmed Cossan's co-worker Andrew Healy. 'I genuinely think he's of the belief that the more he talks about it, the less real the fact he's from Ardkeen will feel.'

While the same reality is something Irish-based English Premier League fans woke up to only recently, it

appears Cossan remains intent on trying to transform into an American.

'Patriots. Don't care what anyone says. It's the Patriots for the Lombardi in 2019,' Cossan said, shouting out into the open-plan office he works in. Visibly sad no one suddenly emerged to hand him an American passport, the Waterford man remained unable to contend with the fact he actually

lives in Ireland and would be eating in Supermac's, not an Arby's or a Wendy's.

UPDATE: Sources close to Cossan have alleged he is now asking people to 'pre-game' at his apartment for the next round of NFL games and will, without question, spend the week searching for American-style red plastic cups.

HORSE RACING

'IT WAS EITHER RUN REALLY FAST ALL MY LIFE, OR BE SLAUGHTERED': CHELTENHAM WINNER

RACEHORSE Sausage Roll obliterated the competition to gain a fifth victory in the Glenfarclas Cross Country Chase at Cheltenham yesterday and is now tipped for the Grand National. But what makes the eight-year-old stand out from the rest? WWN travelled to his stables to chat racing, life and his future plans.

'I suppose growing up with the constant fear of being sent to the slaughterhouse for meat was one of my main motivations,' Sausage Roll began, tucking into a bag of nuts following his win yesterday. 'It was either run really fucking fast all my life or be destroyed by the stud farm.'

Spending most of his younger years on a stud farm in County Tipperary, Sausage Roll detailed a tragic youth, growing up where literally thousands of his friends and family members didn't make the cut.

'When you see your half-sisters and brothers being loaded into

> ### 'Growing up with the constant fear of being sent to the slaughterhouse for meat was one of my main motivations'

the back of a horsebox, knowing they're going on a cramped boat to Belgium, France or Italy to be killed for consumption, you start to realise that there might be something in this running around a track thing, with a little man on your back whipping you,' the horse continued, referring to the 22,000 horses that have been slaughtered by the Irish racehorse industry since 2016.

By the time Sausage Roll turned five, he was one of the country's biggest names in the game, winning race after race both here and in the UK, but he insists he never let the fame go to his head.

'To be honest, I don't get treated any differently. I'm shoved on a cold plane every week and made run like a lunatic every day,' Sausage Roll explained, a giant tear streaming down his face. 'I'd give anything to be grazing and just running free in the wild. Instead, I'm making money for some corrupt sport fuelled by gambling addiction, with the added chance of being shot if I break my leg.'

Sausage Roll is due to race in the Grand National at Aintree in April, before retiring and being sold to an Irish slaughterhouse later next year.

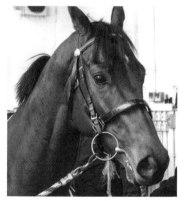

JÜRGEN KLOPP GIVEN SCOUSE ACCENT IN MOVING CEREMONY

IN a ceremony to mark the high esteem in which he is held in Liverpool, manager Jürgen Klopp has been granted the freedom of the Scouse accent.

The German is now free to use the Scouse accent at any time, as Liverpudlians have crafted him a unique accent, which protects him from any dirty looks or criticism in the event of him choosing to enter into an impromptu session of repeating 'Calm down, calm down'.

Klopp, a Champions-League-winning manager, achieved legendary status in the Merseyside club after leading them to a 2-0 victory over Spurs, and said he is truly humbled by the gesture that highlights the special bond forged between him and the fans.

'It's dead sound of 'em, ja'know like. It's brilliant, really, like. Chuffed, aren't I?' Klopp said, in a voice that closely resembled Donald Duck trying to regurgitate some food.

Gone is Klopp's trademark booming Germanic English, which has now, with the permission of the city he coaches in, become something much less easy to understand and quite grating on the ear.

'I just hope I can continue to keep the faith shown to me by the fans,' an emotional Klopp concluded, sounding like a chainsaw in a washing machine being put through a wood chipper.

📺 TV guide

Oh, What's the Point? You're All on Fucking Netflix: RTÉ One, RTÉ2, Virgin Media One and TG4 just fucking give up and go blank for a few hours, fed up with how disloyal their viewers have become.

COPING WITH A CHILD WHO HAS AN INTEREST IN PLAYING SPORTS

IT can be one of the most devastating things to happen a parent – the realisation that one or more of their kids has an interest in playing football with the local side, or taking part in athletics, kickboxing or GAA. For a parent, their whole world can come crashing down the moment their child turns to them and tells them that they would like to start training with their friends every Saturday morning.

No more lie-ins; no more getting good and fucked up on a Friday night, safe in the knowledge that Saturday morning is free for hangover time. There's a lot to deal with when kids start playing sports, so here's a few tips to help you through.

1. It's nobody's fault
It's human instinct to look for someone to blame when a child takes an interest in sport. Some parents blame themselves, and some even harbour feelings of anger toward their child. In actual fact, there's nobody to blame. This is just something that happens to families. It cannot be predicted or prevented. It's best just to come to terms with it and move on.

2. Seek help from friends and family
Tight-knit families with a good network of friends cope best when there's a child in the house who wakes up one morning and thinks he's fucking Messi or something. Having the ability to call on a neighbour and say 'Hey, I'm hungover to bits this morning. Can you take Pippa to camogie?' will prove invaluable over the coming years. Calling in the child's godparents to come take them to training or attend shitty little five-a-side mini-leagues on bank-holiday weekends will also help take the sting

'It's okay, son. You did your best. Sure what does it matter that your best is nowhere near good enough?'

out of you being the only person put out by all this. Share the misery.

3. Encourage the child to just quit
Over time, the child may decide to stop going to training because it's boring, or because they're shit and they don't want to try any harder. It's up to parents to get their kids to this point as quickly as they can. Sow seeds of doubt in your child's mind: 'It's okay, son. You did your best. Sure what does it matter that your best is nowhere near good enough?' This is the only way you will be able to get your kid to stay at home and play Xbox all weekend, leaving you free to enjoy yourself. Jesus Christ, you don't ask for much, like. One day in the week – that's all. One day in the goddamn week. Fuck, like.

RUGBY

COMMON PERSON UNDER IMPRESSION HE CAN LIKE RUGBY, TOO

A common-as-fuck, lower-middle-class type who doesn't live in an affluent area is, for some reason, under the impression that he has as much right as anyone else to enjoy this weekend's rugby clash between Ireland and New Zealand, WWN has learned.

Derek Carron, 47, is looking forward to watching the match with his pals in a frightfully common pub, despite the fact that he earns less than 45k a year and lives in an apartment that he rents – an apartment his dad doesn't even own.

Frequently drawing disgusted looks from the people who surround him at the few rugby matches he can afford to attend with his unattractive, age-appropriate wife and their non-pony-riding kids, Carron has become a figure of scorn among real rugger fans who see him as a 'blemish on the game'.

'Look, there's plenty of GAA games he could go to … Christ, there's the League of Ireland, where he's far more suited,' said one genuine rugby fan we spoke to, leaning on his Audi outside his red-brick Dublin home.

'I've watched him a few times – he doesn't even sing "Ireland's Call". He doesn't drink Heino. He doesn't even have a double-barrelled surname, the fucker. Like, he literally only has one surname.

'Listen, pal. I'm sure there's a pub on the northside that's showing the darts. Head up there if you can get through the police cordon. Be among your people.'

The Irish team has also stated that they're aware of Carron's presence in the stadium, with several players adding that they have a lot of sympathy for the semi-impoverished fan.

'God love him,' said one player. 'I might even give him a jersey at the end.'

Fullmindness

Try 'negitating'. It's like meditating, only you reflect on how you will strike down all your enemies.

DECLAN RICE DUMPS IRELAND DAY BEFORE VALENTINE'S DAY

HEARTLESS footballer Declan Rice heartlessly broke the hearts of Ireland today with a heartlessly well-worded and perfectly reasoned, if disappointing, official statement in which he confirmed he would be dumping the nation the day before Valentine's Day.

Insiders with a closer understanding of Rice's thinking have confirmed he felt Irish football fans came on way too strong, ultimately pushing the 20-year-old footballer away, who was reluctant to take the relationship to the 'next level'.

'My boo, my beau, my bae. How could he do this?' asked a distraught Ireland, who, if it was being honest, knew long ago that Rice was way out of Ireland's league.

After collecting itself, Ireland admitted Rice's recent behaviour made a little more sense now, as he had seemed distant and uninterested for some time.

'We can change, you don't have to do this. Please, Deccy, my little bowl of rice, please,' Ireland called out, knowing full well it couldn't change its overbearing and obsessive ways.

Running through the five stages of grief in a maddening ten seconds, Ireland, clearly hurt, began lashing out.

'The day before Valentine's Day. Really? Oh fine, enjoy your slutty England. But it won't worship you like we did when you glided all over our green grass,' Ireland cried out.

Calming itself down, Ireland unfollowed Rice on Instagram despite

knowing that after a few glasses of wine tomorrow night, it would be prowling social media for pictures of Rice with England, only serving to deepen its heartache.

HURLING

NINE THINGS THAT COULD MAKE HURLING EVEN MORE EXCITING

THE heartpounding spectacle that is hurling doesn't need any more excitement injected into proceedings, but that hasn't stopped us here at WWN Sport from trying.

We've consulted fans, pundits, our one American cousin who's never heard of hurling, as well as ex-players, current players and referees, and formulated nine additions, tweaks and changes that could elevate hurling to an even higher level.

1.Set hurls on fire
Petrol. Matches.

2. Fan cannon
Instead of a sin bin, how about a 'fan cannon'? It would fire, via the cannon, a particularly vocal fan from the sidelines, giving them the opportunity to play for two minutes before being hauled off. These fans are usually overweight and out of shape, so they will add nothing in terms of quality, but the entertainment value is too good to turn down.

3. A third goal
Increased chaos equals greater excitement. The third goal will be facing side on and stationed on the halfway line. Which team is meant to defend it? And who's supposed to be attacking it? Who knows? Let's leave that as a surprise.

4. Occasional two points awarded for over-the-bar scores
But only for ones from waaaaay out that make commentators and supporters say 'Fuck me, that was class.'

5. Put a restraining order out on Sky Sports
Fairly straightforward.

6. More fire
That's right. Keep the flow of petrol that's fuelling the hurl's fire going and going.

7. Even more fire
Jesus, this has got out of hand, lads. D'ya think we should stop?

8.Goal posts, too
I'm really not sure we should set the goals, of all things, on fire because ...

9. Umpires, too
Oh God, what have we done?!

DISAPPOINTMENT AS TAYLOR FAILS TO GET ARRESTED AFTER WINNING THIRD WORLD TITLE

KATIE Taylor has been criticised for undoing all the hard work invested in securing an unprecedented third world title on Friday night in Philadelphia after it emerged the Bray native failed to get arrested.

An act which is the clearest indication yet that the Olympic gold medalist simply has no interest in being celebrated and feted on either the home or international stage, Taylor remained humble in the aftermath of her victory, and refused to rule in the idea of causing criminal damage or spending the night in a cell.

'Does she want to be remembered at all as an absolute legend?' queried one man wearing a singlet who seemed very agitated at the news. 'How can anyone take her seriously now? She's letting down her fans and, more importantly, people who would

be her fans if she just went out and fucked shit up.'

The now IBF, WBA and WBO World Lightweight Champion stopped Rose Volante by TKO but veteran fight-game experts have suggested her insistence on keeping herself to herself will tarnish her reputation forever.

'How many pro fights has it been now? There's not even a hint that she's planning on calling an opponent a Nazi or a faggot. I can see no option other than retirement for her. There's no place in the sport for a humble person like this who just lets their talent do the talking. It's pitiful to watch,' shared one critic.

Elsewhere, parents of young children have vowed to never again let their children watch Taylor in action as the 32-year-old shows no sign of turning into a 'giant arsehole' anytime soon.

BREAKING NEWS

MAN AT CHARITY RUN WITH GOPRO CAMERA MUST BE A PROFESSIONAL OR SOMETHING

OFFICIALS at a local Tramore five-kilometre charity fun run have launched an inquiry after it became apparent that a professional athlete was participating in the field.

The 'Krazy Kostumes Fun Run', in aid of cancer research, was initially billed as a 'family-friendly run for all ages and abilities', while many were encouraged to partake even if they would only walk the 5,000-metre course.

Barry Kearnan, 39, turned up at the starting line armed with a GoPro strapped to his head, sparking rumours that he was an Olympic-level athlete with some grounding in triathlons and endurance events.

'Wow, he looks so impressive with that camera, which I presume

> **'Wow, he looks so impressive with that camera, which I presume will record his run and be beamed back to a huge sports science facility at an elite training facility'**

will record his run and be beamed back to a huge sports science facility at an elite training facility in Oregon, America for closer analysis,' confirmed one onlooker, who was in awe of Kearnan, his midriff slightly exposed thanks to a special, elite

running T-shirt which didn't really fit over his belly.

Race-watchers may have been tempted to interact with Kearnan on the starting line, to ask him questions about Mo Farah, who was probably his training partner, and the upcoming Tokyo 2020 Olympic Games. However, the professional was immersed in testing out his GoPro and making sure it was fully charged.

'Ah, that's okay. His footage will probably be on Eurosport, Sky Sports, RTÉ, CNN and the BBC later. I'll watch him then,' confirmed one run fan.

Kearnan was not believed to be the only professional in the run as another man nearby was stretching his hamstrings while grimacing and grunting intensely.

Health and fitness tip

Looking around the gym to see who's watching you work out can burn an extra 200 calories per hour.

GAELIC FOOTBALL

REVEALED: TEN NEW RULE CHANGES FOR THIS YEAR'S ALL-IRELAND FOOTBALL CHAMPIONSHIP

AFTER the GAA's Standing Committee on the Playing Rules (SCPR) issued a list of proposed experimental rule changes for Gaelic football in early October, the GAA has today revealed ten new changes, after a considerable period of consultation with referees, players and officials.

The SCPR revealed the ten new rules this morning in a press conference at Croke Park, and the following rules have been warmly welcomed by all who love the game dearly, and wish to see the level of play improve for fans and players alike. The rules will first be seen in the Allianz League, before causing huge controversy and stupid debates by the time the championship rolls around.

1. The first punch is free. In all future mass brawls at county and inter-county level, across all age groups, the first punch thrown by a player, umpire or spectator will be a 'free punch', meaning no one can be carded for the offence. Common sense has prevailed on this one.
2. No matter what happens in 2019, Stephen Cluxton will be overlooked for an All Star once

again. Citing the enjoyment that non-Dublin natives get from seeing the imperious keeper being omitted from the All Stars time and time again, the practice will be kept up.
3. The 'hand-pass boredom rule'. A referee may penalise a team when someone in the crowd who is fed up of watching hand-pass after hand-pass screams, 'Ah for fuck sake, what's this boring shite you're at?' at the top of their lungs.
4. Referees will now carry around a Dulux colour wheel pallette. Expanding on the black card, if an elbow to the head or a boot up the hole is deemed not as bad as other offences, referees can consult their colour wheel and award over 400 shades of cards. Also, instead of awarding a red card, which would ruin the game for everyone, they can award a 'rich red', 'ruby red', or similar shade of red which doesn't call for a player's dismissal. A very, very, very, very, very dark grey card will see a player spend two minutes in the sin bin.
5. The sin bin will be run by a local priest, allowing the player the

option to repent their sins during the ten minutes they are in the bin for a black-card offence.
6. To be deemed a foul, a jersey must be fully ripped from the body of an opponent. It is no longer a foul if a player's jersey is only partially torn by an opponent.
7. The words 'Mayo for Sam' have been banned for Mayo's own benefit. The psychological damage each championship has on the people of Mayo is now too grave to be allowed to go on. Thus, standing idly by as delusional people shout 'Mayo for Sam' will no longer be permitted.
8. The 'Joe Brolly mute button'. All games carrying Joe Brolly punditry will automatically come with Brolly muted. If viewers want to listen to hot takes and controversial opinions, they will have to write to RTÉ to formally unmute him.
9. The 'parent-on-the-sideline-sub'. In underage games, any parent talking shit and criticising their child will be given the option of replacing them on the field for the rest of the game, giving them the opportunity to showcase their own lack of stamina, skill and actual knowledge of how to play the game.
10. New rule changes every six weeks. Since there isn't enough tinkering with the rules at the minute, a motion was passed to allow a constant flow of rules being changed every six weeks.

HURLING

LOCAL MAN ASKED TO STOP COMPARING EVERY SPORT TO HURLING

WATERFORD man William Shannon has been begged by family and friends to just try to enjoy sports that aren't hurling, without griping about how the athletes and competitors aren't as hardy as hurlers, or how the action is slow-paced compared to a hotly contested All-Ireland quarter-final where there's 'sliotairs getting leathered around the place'.

Like thousands of people across Ireland, Shannon is so blinded by the skill and toughness of people who play hurling that he has become unable to watch literally any other sport without statements such as 'Those American football lads wouldn't survive a whack of a hurl if they didn't have them big pads on', or 'That cunt wouldn't be that fast if he wasn't on a bicycle.'

Friends of Shannon, 35, have stopped inviting him to the pub with them on Sunday afternoons after growing increasingly tired of having conversations about how Tiger Woods may indeed be a skilled golfer, but he couldn't sink a 15-yard putt 'if there was a lad marking him'.

'It started with soccer, William would be constantly getting angry about lads rolling around looking for penalties,' said one long-suffering pal.

'And then it was rugby. Rugby players don't have the finesse to run 40 yards balancing a ball on a piece of wood no wider than your hand, apparently. After that, literally any sport whatsoever paled in comparison to hurling. We get it, William, you're 100 per cent right. Phil "the Power" Taylor couldn't score 180 if he was getting shoulder-charged while running past the oche. Well done. Now shut the fuck up and let us watch the sport in peace.'

Shannon has reacted to his friend's interview by stating that it lacks the passion and conviction found in a minor hurler being quizzed after a hard-fought victory in a county final against bitter rivals.

KID TAKES FIRST O'NEILLS FOOTBALL TO THE FACE LIKE A TOTAL PRO

WATERFORD boy Jack Lanning has won the admiration of his entire under-10s GAA squad and coaching staff by taking an O'Neills size 4 leather football directly to the face and 'just playing the fuck on'.

Lanning, 9, was at training with his teammates at the weekend when the incident occurred, as he attempted to block a pass from the opposing side at the 45-yard line but inadvertently ended up soaking up the entire impact of the ball with his face, made all the worse by the fact that it happened early in the session and he 'hadn't even had a chance to warm up'.

With everyone expecting the young midfielder to limp off the field after the soaking wet and over-inflated ball smacked into his face with a noise that still rings in the ears of all who witnessed it to this day, Lanning 'totally bossed' the situation by shrugging it off and playing on.

'Everyone knows what it's like to get one of those hard leather bastards right in the face,' said team coach Martin Brennan, wincing at the thought of the impact. 'So we were all prepared for little Jack to have a bit of a cry, lose a bit of respect among his teammates, maybe pick up a name like 'Cry-Ball' that would stay with him for the rest of his adult life, but no, that wee hoor took it full-blast and played on. That's county material right there.'

Lanning's triumphant victory over physics was made all the more impressive later on, when fellow teammate Billy Whelan got a tip – a fucking tip of a ball – and went down home crying like a little bitch.

Animal facts

Birds fly upside down over Dublin because it's not worth shitting on.

MIKE TYSON REASSURES RONALDO EVERYBODY FORGETS ABOUT IT EVENTUALLY

AS reports of rape accusations made against the world's most recognisable athlete, Cristiano Ronaldo, slowly but surely begin to make page 48 of a few newspapers, boxing legend Mike Tyson has spoken publicly to reassure Ronaldo that people just sort of forget about you raping someone when you're famous enough.

Tyson, who was jailed for six years after being found guilty of raping an 18-year-old woman in 1992, found it remarkably easy to be welcomed back into the sporting world once he was released, insisting that most people will forget about it all soon enough, and Ronaldo can just get back to being Ronaldo.

'You'd think people, brands, football clubs and especially fans would take a stand but they don't, and they won't. Yes, it's an incredibly depressing thought, but if I were Ronaldo I wouldn't worry. It'll be fine,' Tyson revealed, in his unmistakable voice that initially entered a 'not guilty' plea in his trial on rape charges, and went on to

'If I were Ronaldo, I'd just be looking forward to starring in *The Hangover Part II*. Just like I did, despite it being well known that I am a convicted rapist'

secure massive paydays in boxing bouts once released from prison.

Despite Nike releasing a statement which saw the company take the allegations against Ronaldo very seriously, Tyson, who has some experience in the field of everyone forgetting about your heinous crimes because you're a marketable star who can make people money, is adamant that rape really isn't something that will stop a career.

'He's probably worried, thinking "God, everyone is going to abandon

me. I'll be fired. I'll go to jail. I'll lose my sponsor deals once people read up on the shocking and horrid details," but trust me, if I were Ronaldo, I'd just be looking forward to starring in *The Hangover Part II*. Just like I did, despite it being well known that I am a convicted rapist,' an affable Tyson reassured.

Elsewhere, Ronaldo's club Juventus has confirmed they are unwilling to read reports about the Portuguese man as they've spent a lot of money on him and it's very important to their brand that he goes on to sell a lot of football jerseys, no matter what he may have done a million years ago in 2009.

GAELIC FOOTBALL

NOVELTY KINDA WEARING OFF, ADMIT DUBS

THE capital headed to bed early last night following the Dublin senior team's fourth consecutive All-Ireland Gaelic football victory, with most fans admitting there was no real cause to stay out celebrating due to the novelty of being champions wearing off.

The Dubs comfortably scooped the game's top prize by beating Tyrone 2-17 to 1-14, in what was described as less of a 'clash' and more of a 'routine trophy awarding'. Thousands of Dublin fans in attendance just sort of nodded along, only looking up from their phones every so often to see how far ahead they were.

Trapped in ennui, the Dublin team headed off early with the Sam Maguire as RTÉ just played the trophy presentation from last year. Stephen Cluxton admitted that he didn't know what more there was to say.

'Yay,' said one Dublin supporter following the final whistle, doing his best to sound enthusiastic.

'Fair play to Tyrone all the same,' said another, trying to make it sound as convincing as he could.

'Same time next year?' sighed another season ticket holder, in anticipation of next year's historic five-in-a-row victory, and six in 2020, seven in 2021, and so on.

'Not these fuckers again,' sighed a kid in Temple Street, as the Dublin team showed up with Sam this morning for a 'surprise' visit.

Meanwhile, the other county teams have settled on a plan of action for next year, which will not involve changing their style of play to emulate the success of the Dubs, but will focus instead on griping about how one team being better than all the others 'isn't fair'.

WWN Was There

𝔚aterford 𝔚hispers News

Arson attack on Roosky hotel, a proposed site for Direct Provision centre, 10 January 2019

What we said then: It's 2019, folks. Can't we just for a moment try and see things from someone else's perspective? Those who are quick to judge call these people racist, but has anyone taken the time to think that maybe they just hate people based on the colour of their skin?

What we say now: Okay, we got this wrong, but who hasn't jumped the gun? How were we to know that the arsonists actually burned down this hotel because it once served them an 'Irish Breakfast' that included black pudding but no white pudding. A simple, non-racist explanation.

GAA

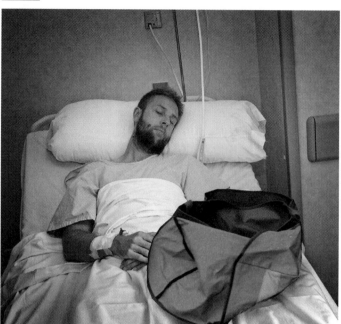

POSTMAN PARALYSED AFTER DELIVERING VALENTINES TO LOCAL GAA STAR

SURGEONS in Westmeath are battling to save the spine of a Mullingar postman who was crushed under the weight of Valentine's Day cards on his way to local GAA hotshot Fintan O'Lough.

Postman Derek Kinghan reportedly suffered a compound fracture of the L1–L5 area of his spine after attempting to lift his postal bag while doing his rounds today.

It is believed that the sheer number of cards and gifts being sent to St Phelim Gaels corner-forward

O'Lough caused the postman to literally compress under their sheer weight, but the county-bound football star has yet to accept any responsibility.

'Look, it's not my fault that I get so many Valentine's cards. I'm just a damn handsome bastard who on average knocks over 2-14 from play every time I step onto a damn pitch,' said O'Lough, spraying himself with his fourth can of Lynx today.

'What I want to know is why wasn't this postman prepared for the weight of his bag? He knows I'm on his route. He should have expected that I'd be getting thousands of cards and little bears and things today. Bend with your knees, man, you're heading to the O'Lough house in time for V-Day. Dude should have been doing squats since Christmas in preparation.'

PROUD LOCAL FATHER VERBALLY ABUSING REFEREE AT SON'S FOOTBALL GAME

A local father bursting with pride due to his son's exploits on the football pitch has once again taken to calling a referee a 'blind cunt' who he will 'see after the game' to 'straighten him out', WWN can reveal.

'Aw, isn't that lovely? Such a supportive father who isn't creating any lasting psychological trauma for his son,' observed someone out walking their dog near where the under-9 match between Ballyfinn Rovers and Ardbreen FC was being played.

Anthony Shields, 39, proud as punch of his son Conor, never misses a game or an opportunity to volley abuse at a referee if they even so much as breathe.

'How is that not a penalty, ref? Where'd you learn to referee, Specsavers? Fucking joke,' added Shields, hoping the referee would tell him to calm down so he could do the opposite.

Shields's parenting skills were much admired by fellow parents on the sideline, who couldn't help but copy and mimic the supportive way he watched his son kick a ball.

'There's something special about that father–son bond, isn't there?' remarked an onlooker who couldn't understand why young Conor said 'I want to go home' at half-time.

'WE ARE NOT BREAKING SPENDING RULES': CONFIRMS GOLD-PLATED MAN CITY SPOKESPERSON

A Manchester City spokesperson made entirely out of gold has rejected in the strongest terms possible claims by *Der Spiegel* newspaper that the club has trodden all over the Financial Fair Play Regulations overseen by UEFA, WWN can confirm.

'Our new endorsement deal from an Abu Dhabi pencil-sharpening manufacturer worth $17 billion each year is yet another example of the prudent revenue-raising business City conducts on a daily basis,' confirmed the spokesperson from atop an eight-foot-high golden plinth.

Glistening under TV studio lights, the spokesperson for the reigning Premier League champions has confirmed all revenue-raising efforts are entirely legitimate and that leaked emails from the club clearly stating otherwise are not true.

'We'd hardly call that evidence,' added the shiny man before pausing to clear his throat, hundreds of thousands of euro spilling from his mouth in the process. 'Sorry, something blocking my throat there.'

The revelations that a high-level club like Man City could be breaking the rules of FFP with the aide of then-UEFA head Gianni Infantino has been greeted with huge outrage and protests from passionate football fans, who are devastated by thoughts that the game they love so much is being corrupted and debased at every turn.

'Meh,' confirmed a large section of football fans, before adding they reckon City will smash Shakhtar Donetsk tonight.

Elsewhere, a player playing for a club in the Faroe Islands league has been banned for life by UEFA, after drinking an energy drink belonging to a non-official UEFA partner.

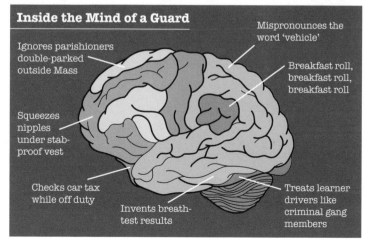

Inside the Mind of a Guard

Ignores parishioners double-parked outside Mass

Mispronounces the word 'vehicle'

Breakfast roll, breakfast roll, breakfast roll

Squeezes nipples under stab-proof vest

Checks car tax while off duty

Invents breath-test results

Treats learner drivers like criminal gang members

EXCLUSIVE

ROY KEANE CONVERTS TO BUDDHISM IN BID TO CURB TEMPER

IN the wake of a fresh row with any number of footballers, Ireland assistant manager Roy Keane has taken the unprecedented step of converting to Buddhism in a bid to finally find some inner calm, WWN can reveal.

With Ireland now resorting to calling up players across the country from the under-9 leagues to fill the increasing number of vacancies in the squad caused by Keane's relentlessly intemperate ways, the Cork man has acknowledged the need for a big life change to curb his temper.

Fullmindness

The path to enlightenment can be found in rejecting capitalism and materialism. To find out more, please sign up to our subscription service for just €20 a month.

> ## I had no idea that meditation involved screaming non-stop while throwing things around'

'Roy's made the decision by himself. I wouldn't push him into anything and, to be fair, whatever works for Roy at the end of the day, as long as he doesn't become one of those self-immolating monks,' confirmed Ireland manager Martin O'Neill, who is without Harry Arter and 945 other Irish players following Keane-related bust ups.

Buddhism, which places personal spiritual development at the centre of its belief system, with followers attempting to achieve inner peace or a state of Nirvana, could be the answer to newly minted monk Keane's quest for calm. The former Man United player was unavailable for interviews with the media, as his new routine requires him to meditate for 22 hours a day.

'I put my ear to the door of his "Room of Calm" just to check up on him,' added O'Neill. 'I had no idea that meditation involved screaming non-stop while throwing things around, but honestly he's like a new man. Fair play to him.'

It's not just O'Neill who seems overjoyed with Roy's conversion, as the players he coaches are already heaping praise on him.

'So basically, lads, Roy's got back from a pilgrimage to Bhutan. The training is better, the lads all seem in a happier mood. There's less tension and, oh, Roy is wearing full Buddhist robes and has rejected all forms of materialism. He hasn't called anyone an "injury-stricken cunt" today. So far so good,' confirmed an Irish squad insider in a WhatsApp voice message which leaked to the press.

MIXED MARTIAL ARTS

'SORRY': MCGREGOR APOLOGISES TO FANS FOR MARCHING WITH VARADKAR

PART-TIME UFC fighter Conor McGregor has apologised today for marching side by side with Irish leader Leo Varadkar, stating he was 'unaware' the Taoiseach was going to be attending the Chicago Saint Patrick's Day parade and that he was 'truly embarrassed' by the whole fiasco.

With the Irish embassy in Chicago seeking answers as to how the world champion fighter was hoodwinked into marching with Ireland's most-hated man in the city's famous Saint Patrick's Day parade, fears have been sparked that the 30-year-old's career may be now tarnished as a result.

'If I knew he was going to be there I would have pulled out straight away,' a rather red-faced McGregor told the press this morning, using the sort of accent one uses when talking to foreigners. 'I've a reputation to keep up here. There's 10,000 people homeless back home because of his government and he cares very little for my fan base, as most of them earn below the living wage.

'This mistake could crush me and all I can say to my fans is that I'm truly sorry. He just seemed to sneak in there. I'm absolutely devastated.'

Taoiseach Varadkar and Minister for Rural Development Michael Ring were not available for comment on their sudden appearance, but it is understood organisers of the event have since apologised to the McGregor team for the mix-up.

'We pass on our sincere apologies to Conor and his fans for not researching Mr Varadkar's failings as a leader. We hope this does not affect his future career in any way,' the brief apology stated.

Bill's Campaign Diary

Veteran journalist Bill Badbody takes a leave of absence from his day-to-day reporting at WWN HQ to pursue a career in politics, in the hope of securing a place as MEP in the European elections. This is his story.

Week 9

Election week and RTÉ, Virgin, TG4, Newstalk and TodayFM have all blocked me on Twitter. It's time to drain the entire bog – media included. I'll close them all down once in Europe. They'll pay, every single last one of them rotten bastards.

After 20 years of marriage, Anne sent me our first-ever sex text. Who'd have thought she was so filthy and graphic? 'Loved the nipple clamps last night' is obviously code for something. I don't even have a 'circumcised cock', but look it, I'll take whatever sex texting I can get at this age. Had to google 'exotic fuck puppet' too. I can't wait to make sweet, sweet love to her when she gets home from her exercise trip. Heat obviously making her horny.

Two days to go and Fiachra's phone going straight to voicemail? EU must have got to him too as he keeps sending me the same text message 'Looking for wages'. This doesn't sound like him. Fiachra wouldn't turn on me like that. Not now. Not over a measly four grand.

That's the fourth time now I've seen that helicopter today. Phone also making strange beeping noise when ringing Fiachra. They're listening. Swept the house for bugs. Lined the study in aluminium foil. If I'm missing tomorrow you will know they've got to me. Sleeping in wardrobe tonight, just to be safe.

Voting tomorrow and it's just me here for the last day of the elections. Talks of a broadcast ban so hired a plane to drag the words 'VOTE BILL NO.1' across the Dublin sky. I will not be silenced. Seems like the exit polls have been rigged by the left-wing mainstream media trying to influence voters tomorrow. Says I've a 0 per cent vote. You're not going to pull that old trick on Bill, *Irish Times*.

Classifieds

Weetabix Bowl Washer Sought: Washer needed to clean over 500 bowls caked in Weetabix. We're sick of buying new bowls but just couldn't be arsed trying to scrape the residue off ourselves as we're a very busy family. Experience using jackhammer essential. Full-time job. Must be able to reach under children's beds to retrieve bowls.

Contact Tracey, 01 3765 4678.

WOMEN PLAY SPORTS, TOO – AND OTHER LESSONS THE MEDIA TAUGHT US IN 2019

The media has always been at the forefront of knowing things and 2019 was no different when it came to the sporting press, as they recently discovered you haven't been reporting on women's sports enough.

Many media outlets took a long, hard look at everybody but themselves when trying to figure out who was to blame for their refusal to grant greater prominence to female sportspeople in their sports sections. It turns out that it was the fault of their readers all along.

In fact, women playing sport was a big revelation which was uncovered by sections of the sports press, who couldn't believe supporters weren't sending journalists to cover female athletes.

'Wow, it's about time, guys,' retorted newspaper sports editors around the country, who couldn't believe it took you this long to support sportswomen here and abroad. You should be truly ashamed.

The women's football World Cup was also invented this year, much to the surprise of fans who could have sworn they wrote letters to broadcasters in the past asking why they didn't deem it worthy of proper coverage.

Looking ahead to 2020, the media sincerely hopes you've learned your lesson, and that you welcome all the uplifting videos, articles and podcasts it bestows upon you, even though you never gave women in a sport a second thought.

RUGBY

STREET LITTERED WITH HANDBAGS FOLLOWING RUGBY BRAWL

BLACKROCK residents were left picking up the pieces this morning following a late-night brawl between rival rugby fans, which left the streets littered with various styles of expensive handbags.

On Tuesday night a number of videos showing a group of young men breaking into a fight outside a pub in the south Dublin village began to appear across various social media platforms.

'I seen one well-nourished young man wearing a Terenure College jersey with the collar up smashing a Louis Vuitton bag off another,' one eyewitness recalled. 'Then another similar-looking guy called Fiachra began joining in with his Michael Kors, sending concealer make-up all over the street. It was actually very entertaining.'

It is estimated that over €10,000 worth of handbags were left on the bloodless streets following the incident, with locals calling on more gardaí to be stationed in the area.

'Someone could have lost an eyeliner, or burst a moisturiser bottle,' insisted Blackrock busybody Sheila O'Neill. 'How many more handbags will we see on our streets before someone gets seriously hurt?'

Fortunately, the clean-up operation was quite fast, with many locals chipping in to pick up the debris.

Suburban Dictionary

'Eh', 'ah' and 'um':
Sounds used to take a brief but important rest from speaking and communicating clearly.

w w news

Waterford Whispers News

TRENDING

RELATIONSHIPS

GUIDE TO DATING IF YOU'RE A MISERABLE CUNT

MORE and more tight-fisted Irish people are having to choose between the sting of loneliness and the sting of paying for a night out, as the dating scene in Ireland strays further and further away from just shifting the nearest person to you in a nightclub ten minutes before it closes, WWN can reveal.

If you're pining for the love of a good woman or man, but you're also a miserable skinflint who hates paying for anything, there may be a few things you can do to make sure the transition from stranger to partner costs you as little as possible:

1. Fun dates during the day
You don't have to take a date to the cinema or to a restaurant. You can have just as good a time at a free event, such as a walk in the park, or sitting on a bench beside a river. Maybe you and your new companion could go to the beach, or hike in a forest. Just remember to bring a two-litre bottle of tap water with you in case they say they're thirsty, hinting that they may want to stop at a shop and buy an expensive bottle of something. Not today, Satan!

2. Cut to the chase
Part of the fun of dating is spending time with a wide range of people, until you find someone who you really click with. But that can involve a lengthy and expensive process where each date will expect to be brought somewhere – not great if you're keeping a tight eye on your ever-dwindling Communion money. So before you bring someone to a restaurant, just cut right to the point. Is this going anywhere? Do you see them as a potential soulmate? If not, why are you wasting 40 quid on a trip to the cinema midweek? Save yourself some serious wallet-ache by coming right out from day one. If they tell you to fuck off, well, at least you'll know.

3. Consider dying alone
They say there's somebody out there for everyone. Maybe this just isn't true. If you haven't found that special person that fits all your criteria (attractive, good fun, great personality, doesn't live anywhere that requires a toll to be paid while driving there), then why put yourself into financial discomfort trying? Loneliness isn't ideal, but it costs fuck all! Jump on the lonely train! Toot toot!

Fullmindness
Suffer from anxiety? Talk to a friend who doesn't have it and they'll help you solve it by simply telling you to 'relax'.

SOCIAL MEDIA

ARE YOUR PARENTS SAFE ONLINE?

KIDS! Do you know what your parents are up to when they go online? A startling new study shows that almost 100 per cent of parents are exposing themselves to fake news, spam articles, endless clickbait holes and arguments with Russian spambots every time they surf the information superhighway – often with disastrous results.

Concerned? You should be. Here are a few pointers to help keep your old ones safe:

1. Talk to them

Rather than being critical of your parents' online activity, it's better to sit them down and talk to them. Find out what they have been searching for online, and talk them through the things they have seen. Make them aware of the fact that what they post online is there for ever, and encourage them to think before they make a comment on a 'Liberal dot ie' post about black taxi drivers using fake Hailo accounts to steal wheelchairs from old folks' homes.

Animal facts

A group of swallows is called a flight; a group of Irish politicians is called a disappointment.

2. Don't let them have access to the Internet in their rooms

If your parents must have the Internet, then it should be at a designated time, in a communal area of your home. Until they can be trusted not to sign up for an alt-right march posing as 'Justice for Ireland' or some shit like that, their Internet access should be both restricted and heavily monitored.

3. Be aware of their social media habits

Many old people can become angry and confused on social media, causing them to lash out at younger people and make total dicks of themselves.

Although it may be a breach of child–parent trust, you have a duty to take a sneaky look at their Facebook and Twitter accounts when they're not in the room. Their password will be either the home phone number or the word 'password', so it shouldn't be too hard.

4. Explain to them that there are no Hot Russian MILFs in the area

They've lived in a bungalow down a boreen their whole lives. They know everyone in the parish. If there was a Russian MILF living just 1.4 km away, she'd be in the kitchen having tea right now. Put the keyboard down, Dad.

MOTORING

ACCELERATING AT A MOTORIST TRYING TO PULL OUT ONTO THE ROAD: A GUIDE

SOME drivers believe they can just calmly pull out onto a street or road without any permission from approaching motorists and expect not to be accelerated at. Well, WWN is here to counteract this terrible assumption with some neat acceleration tips to frighten the absolute shite out of them.

Expensive cars that are better than yours are the biggest culprits for pulling out from parking spaces and expecting to join your traffic queue, so always make sure to never, ever let those bastards pull out, despite how far away and safe a distance they may be from your car.

If you have to, break the local 50 km/h speed limit and force your fellow motorist to double-think their manoeuvre. You're in charge here and you'll decide whether they can or cannot enter the current traffic flow.

Always have your index finger on the headlights while you're accelerating, just in case they are going to double-bluff your obvious acceleration. Yes, you were initially at a safe distance for them to pull out, but that's not the point. Now that you've accelerated, they're not, so they're wrong and should in no way have called your bluff. Cheeky bastards.

If they persist despite your threatening attempt, make sure to have your foot ready for an overly dramatic brake. Practise your 'Ah, for fuck sake' face in the mirror if you have to. Throw your two hands in the air for effect. That's it, show them how angry you are for adding 0.007 of a second to your journey time. Pricks.

If all that fails and they've managed to squeeze out in front of you, make sure to stare at them angrily in their rearview mirror while tailgating them for the remainder of their time in front of you. This will make sure they will never pull out onto the road or street without your permission, ever again.

Repeat every time.

Fullmindness

If someone suddenly pulls out in front of you while driving, don't beep. Simply smile and carry on like nothing happened. Then follow them home and burn down their house.

HEALTH

FIVE WAYS YOU CAN GET RID OF YOUR DISGUSTING FLAB, YOU FAT PIG

Health and fitness tip

Intermittent fasting every leap year can reset your body back to before you were born.

HAVING spent the run-up to Christmas running articles on festive food, drinks, restaurants and treats for you to enjoy, it's now time for us to push articles at you showing how you can shed the pounds of disgusting fat you've packed onto yourself, so that you can rejoin civilisation without bringing shame down on your entire family. Let's get you less jiggly, piggly!

1. Go vegan
Remember that 'Top 5 Restaurants You Must Try This Winter' article we published in December? You may be confusing it with the 'Top 5 Restaurants You Must Try This December', 'Top 5 Restaurants You Must Try This Christmas', 'Top 5 Restaurants You Must Try This Yuletide', or 'Top 5 Restaurants You Must Try During the Season of Boreas, Greek God of the Cold North'. Anyway, forget what we said in those. Get your fat arse some vegetables and soy milk. Not sure where to get such things? Don't worry, we'll be running 'Top 5 Vegan Restaurants You Must Try' and 'This Dublin Vegan Supermarket is Fucking Amazing' articles for the next month.

2. Try these dietary supplements
In the run-up to Christmas, we teamed up with loads of supermarket chains and restaurants to bring you sponsored content, selling you everything from Christmas chocolates to Christmas eels. We're super happy with the results of our targeted media performance during this time, and it's clear from your fat face that they proved very effective. Now we're teaming up with a chain of dietary supplement shops for all your

meal-replacement bar and meal-replacement shake needs. And boy, do you need them.

3. Run
Hmm … Not sure about this one. Running is more or less free – you could do it right now if you wanted. If you have feet and a road, that's about it. Not sure how we could profit from this just yet … Maybe wait until we link up with a chain of gyms or something like that, so that we can get commission from your membership when you join up. We'll need to create some content around this. Maybe a quick '5 Tips' video shot in a branch of a chain gym, dictated by one of Ireland's fittest and most affordable Instagram models. Bear with us on this one.

4. Buy *January Diets Made Easy* by Saoirse Zarnell
You may have never heard of Saoirse Zarnell, but she's everywhere. The social media sensation has just released her first book and it's packed with tips and recipes that someone else collated for her. Really, all they did was take 100 pages of recipes, added in 50 pages of Saoirse doing lunges in a Lycra top, and stuck in a picture of her blending kale while smiling in a kitchen that's bigger than the house you grew up in. You're going to be seeing a lot of Saoirse Zarnell over the next 12 months. We're going to make damn sure of it. From her upcoming break-up with one of the lads from some band you've never heard of, to her ongoing work raising awareness for something you're already aware of, we're going to load you with Saoirse Zarnell until you crack the fuck up. Get a head start now by buying her book and shedding your hideousness. You'll never achieve her body – not unless your only job is to do yoga and eat air all day – but at least having the book in your house will make visitors think that you're trying. Get 10 per cent off when you use our offer code FATFUCK.

5. Enhance your mental well-being
A fit mind means a fit body. Probably. We're not sure there's science to back that up, but it sounds good. Download our mindfulness app and relax while simultaneously listening to our mindfulness podcast. You can do it. We're here to help you! We believe in you now, just like we believed in you in December when we showed you how it was empowering to eat a whole tub of Celebrations in one sitting, or when we brought you ads for that sweet deal that got you six bottles of prosecco for €23. You can do it, fatty! And if you can't do it now, we'll run this article again in time for summer!

SOCIAL MEDIA

XTREME COMMENTING: THE PEOPLE RISKING EVERYTHING TO TALK ABOUT SENSITIVE ISSUES ONLINE

FORGET BASE jumping and motocross. Put away your skateboards and your BMX bicycles. Take down your posters of Tony Hawk and Evel Knievel. There's a new extreme sport in town, and it's only open to the craziest bastards alive today – Xtreme commenting.

Whereas Evel only risked his ability to walk when he jumped over the fountains at Caesars Palace, and Felix Baumgartner only risked his ability to be alive when he skydived from outer space, Xtreme commenters risk their livelihoods, their reputations and their personal safety with each comment they post online, risking it all to join in the conversation on some of the most sensitive subjects around today.

The margin for error when discussing these subjects online is about the same as French daredevil Philippe Petit had when he infamously walked a tightrope between the towers of the World Trade Center – fuck all.

Far from being far-right nutjobs who just spout shite and walk away unscathed from the fallout, many Xtreme commenters are naturally left-leaning liberals who gained entry into the sport by commenting in agreement with people on a number of sensitive subjects, only to find that their views and comments were not 100 per cent aligned with whoever was most vocal about the subject at the time.

Amazed at the sheer insanity of anyone who would willingly post a comment about any sensitive subject online, WWN sat down with one Waterford-based Xtreme commenter as she prepared for her riskiest comment yet: a tweet about a subject so dangerously sensitive that we dare not even mention it here.

'People ask skydivers why they'd jump out of a perfectly good aeroplane, and people ask me why I'd risk my entire well-being going anywhere near this discussion,' said Ellen Harris, one of Ireland's best-known Xtreme commenters.

'Every time I hit send, it's just an adrenaline shot to the heart. Just like any extreme sport, you can have your equipment checked, you can have your research and your planning done, you can be as 'right' and on the side of justice and fair play as you believe it's possible to be, and then just … BAM. You're done. You misspoke. You used a term that became insensitive last week when you weren't looking. You're fucked. Emails get sent to your place of work. Your reputation is in tatters. Maybe death threats, who knows? You're cancelled.'

Harris went on to further explain the risks that Xtreme commenters take everytime they post anything online, including the sheer dread that one of your worst enemies might agree with you and RT your post.

'You post something you think is a clever and ironic tweet about people who are anti-immigration, and then fucking Katie Hopkins gives you a thumbs up. That's … a tough way to spend an evening, trying to convince a thousand angry people that you're on their side while they go through your Timeline to find shit to tear you down with.

'Ordinary people get around this by just keeping their mouths shut, never adding to any debate or discussion online. When they see the fucking train wrecks that some people get into at the hands of people they should be natural allies with, it's hard to blame them.'

Harris wrapped up by solemnly accepting that the survival rate for Xtreme commenters was, in her words, 'unenviable'.

'Nobody can be absolutely right online, all the time,' she said sadly, remembering fellow Xtreme commenters who were forced to delete their Twitter accounts after 'shit went down'.

'You post something at night and your life could be over by the time you wake up the next day. The only way to be safe is to say nothing, and stay the fuck away from discussions and causes. People look at me and say they could never be like me. I look at them and say the same thing.'

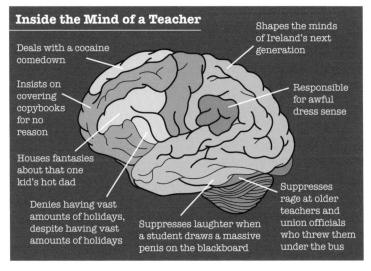

Inside the Mind of a Teacher

Shapes the minds of Ireland's next generation

Deals with a cocaine comedown

Insists on covering copybooks for no reason

Responsible for awful dress sense

Houses fantasies about that one kid's hot dad

Denies having vast amounts of holidays, despite having vast amounts of holidays

Suppresses laughter when a student draws a massive penis on the blackboard

Suppresses rage at older teachers and union officials who threw them under the bus

CLIMATE CHANGE

GUIDE TO IGNORING THE LATEST CLIMATE CHANGE WARNINGS

THE dire prognoses from climate scientists about how we may have a decade or less to save humanity and avert a catastrophic climate-change disaster on Earth has shocked millions into action, with many readers getting in touch with WWN Environment to ask if there is a more effective way to ignore the warnings than by putting their fingers in their ears and yelling.

With irreversible global-warming events kicking off a climate chain reaction resulting in tsunamis, hurricanes, fatal heatwaves and a whole host of other weather events, many people are wondering how best to ignore it all and do nothing because that takes the least effort.

WWN Environment has endeavoured to curate an invaluable guide which can help everyone come together as one with a common purpose and just completely ignore the latest climate-change warnings, which are the most terrifying to ever be issued to the human race.

1. *Ozark* season 2 is out on Netflix

Worth watching if the alternative is boring stuff like having to face up to the fact that climate change won't be reversed unless someone like you starts fighting for it. But look, that's a lot of effort.

2. I'm a farmer

Yup, should be easy enough for you to ignore. In fact, why not lobby the government to let you be even less environmentally friendly but have them pretend those new changes to law and policies are actually 'pro-environment'.

3. Should we do brunch on Sunday at 11 am or 12 pm? Is it lunch if it's at 12 pm?

Yeah, just generally going about your business like the newspapers, newsfeeds and news bulletins aren't filled with explicit warnings that it's now or never if you want to ensure the planet is around and in existence for when your kids are your age.

Oh, and don't forget to pass the blame on to someone else when time officially runs out.

4. Ow, this hurts. It appears the skin is melting off my skull

You did it! You ignored the warnings so well it's now 2041 and oh my fucking God, is it just us or is it skin-meltingly hot?

Fullmindness

Make sure everyone knows of your suffering by constantly sharing anxiety and depression memes online. This will push them away. Do this until everyone mutes you. Enjoy the silence.

TRAVEL

FIVE HOLIDAY DESTINATIONS WHERE KIDS CAN GET SOME GOOD WHINGEING DONE

WITH summer nearly upon us, it's time for families to start thinking about where best to head for their annual holiday. At this stage, it's important to factor into your budget the size of your family, the ages of your children, and the culinary preferences of all involved, to maximise the amount of whingeing you have to sit through in order to return home even more stressed out than when you left.

Need some destination tips? Look no further:

1. Sun holidays

If you're looking for a real all-in destination which almost guarantees kids of all ages have something to complain about, you really can't beat the popular sun, sand and sea holiday packages.

From smaller kids whingeing about having to wear sun lotion to your older kids griping about not being allowed to go off with the local teenagers in the evenings, there's something for all parents to get stressed and angry about.

Whingeing about not being at the beach,

whingeing about being at the beach too long, whingeing about it being too hot, whingeing about sand in their €4 ice-cream – these trips are all but guaranteed to make you wish you were back in work.

2. City breaks

If your kids aren't the type to complain about too much sun, then they're certainly the type to complain about too much boredom, and nothing will bring that out of them quite like a getaway in any major city.

Pisa to Paris, Barcelona to Budapest, cities are full of beautiful museums, sights and bistros that will have your kid grousing about being bored, to the point where you'll quickly wonder why you didn't just stay at home and do up the garden instead of wasting a month's wages on this bullshit.

> **These trips are all but guaranteed to make you wish you were back in work.**

> **'Your kids, a tent, no WiFi, no McDonald's, no Fortnite, no dry clothes … Yes, that'll do just nicely. Get ready to hear not just pissing, but pissing and moaning'**

3. Theme parks

Surely you can't go wrong with a theme park, right? With rides, parades and attractions galore, theme parks across the continent are perfect for keeping

your kids glowing with excitement for at least an hour, until the hassle of queuing, your insistence at keeping them by your side, and your firm stance on not buying them a €12 tub of popcorn bring about the classic whinges that you yourself put your parents through when they brought you on holiday. Karma doesn't take a vacation, pal.

4. Camping

Yup, that'll do it. Your kids, a tent, no WiFi, no McDonald's, no Fortnite, no dry clothes … Yes, that'll do just nicely. Get ready to hear not just pissing, but pissing and moaning. And if you double up on camping at a music festival, you get to enjoy it, all the while being kind of stoned but not stoned enough, along with the withering looks of everyone as they wonder why the fuck you brought your kids to Electric Picnic.

5. Staycation

Stay at home. See if that changes anything. You think you can escape a summer of whingeing just by going nowhere? You think your kids aren't going to whinge in the house, or in the paddling pool out the back that took you three hours and your last breath to blow up? These are your kids, right? You didn't just find them somewhere.

DON'T LIKE MILLENNIALS? THEN YOU'LL HATE THESE LITTLE BASTARDS

WHEN it comes to laying blame on someone for the current state of the world, millennials are the perfect group to point the finger at. They're young and whiny, they all seem to be fairly good looking and they all have it much better than we did, and you never hear us complain.

From driving up house prices with their avocado toast to single-handedly wrecking the economy by misappropriating what they did with their Communion money, millennials have taken a perfectly good world with a fully functioning monetary system and a just, honest and fair parliamentary process that ensured equal rights for everyone and just, well … They just fucked it all up, didn't they?

With today's current crop of young folk getting too old to just sit back and let everyone blame them for the state of the place, fears were growing that perhaps blame might shift on to older generations. Luckily, there's a new batch of

'There's a generation of kids that are about to be born – some of them are already here – and they're going to be responsible for everything bad over the next 20 years'

babies, some not even born yet, and just you wait until you see how they're going to fuck up the world.

'Millennials? You ain't seen nothing yet,' said World Blame co-ordinator Pierce Winglan, looking at a wall covered in ultrasound pictures.

'There's a generation of kids that are about to be born – some of them are already here – and they're going to be responsible for everything bad over the next 20 years. Massive economic recessions, that's their fault. Soaring oil prices, more bloodshed in

the Middle East, you can blame this lot. Just look at them up there, with their smartphones and their fucking … umbilical cords. No regard or respect for older generations. You can rest assured they'll be pointing the finger at us going "Wah, why did you vote this way?", "Wah, why did you sell the planet for a handful of magic beans, leaving us with nothing except sickness and poverty?" … Fucking state of them, they make me want to puke.'

Millennials themselves are looking forward to the arrival of the new batch of scapegoats, with many admitting that while they feel bad about blaming the next generation for everything, it's just nice to be out of the crossfire for once.

Community text alerts

Everyone to receive new purple, orange and red bins this week. No idea what they're for.

MOTORING

GUIDE TO WALKING BEHIND A REVERSING CAR LIKE A BIG FUCKING EEJIT

HAVE you ever seen a car moving in a backwards motion and thought, 'I'd love to just walk out in front of that car like a big fucking eejit'? Neither have we, but WWN has created a guide on how to do it anyway in the hopes that natural selection will one day curb our ever-spiralling population.

Location is everything with this feat, so we would suggest finding a nice, busy supermarket car park to target. Multistorey car parks are not as good as people are a lot more cautious, so if you can find a flat car park at a Tesco or a Lidl, you're sure to score.

We would also suggest waiting for days with poor visibility, where the car windows fog up easily and people are in more of a rush to get home.

Once the location and climate is perfect, you need to search for cars

> **No matter what the outcome, whether you've been hit, run over, or the driver has seen you in time, just stare at them like they're the ones who are in the wrong**

parked facing inwards, so the back is out on the road area of the car park. Remember, white lights mean the car is in reverse. The second big giveaway is the fact the car is moving in a backwards motion, as opposed to a forward motion. NOTE: Never walk out in front of a forward-moving car as

the driver will only see you and stop, ruining your little surprise.

Now, once happy you've spotted a car in a reversing motion, calmly walk right in its fucking way. Seriously, don't even think about this. Just do it. It's up to the driver to stop moving, not you, even though you're on the road area and shouldn't be there and the driver won't have a leg to stand on in court. NOTE: You may also not have a leg to stand on following this, but that's a more literal thing than legal.

No matter what the outcome, whether you've been hit, run over, or the driver has seen you in time, just stare at them like they're the ones who are in the wrong, and not you for basically walking in front of a moving vehicle.

You're welcome.

RELATIONSHIPS

HOW TO MAINTAIN A LONG-DISTANCE RELATIONSHIP BY RIDING ALL AROUND YOU

WITH thousands of couples across Ireland in long-distance relationships due to work or college requirements, 'How do you keep your sex life alive?' is the question that most relationship experts get asked. Well, one Waterford couple counsellor may have stumbled upon a solution to the problem. Simply ride everything you can while your partner is away.

'There are partners, married couples, even just young couples who are separated for weeks, even months at a time, all wondering how they can preserve the physical side of their relationship,' said Dr Cathal Barron, one of Waterford's leading experts on hole-getting.

'A lot of relationship counsellors would recommend using Skype and the like for sexy chat, sending racy texts and pics to each other. I

> **'Keep your mouth shut, remember to use johnnies and boom, you still have a loving partner who thinks you're being faithful'**

think it's much simpler to just fuck all around you while your partner is away, and say nothing when they get home.'

Although his methods may be controversial, Dr Barron insists that the process is virtually flawless.

'As long as you stay safe, the other party need never know that you've been dipping everything in sight while they're off working in Canada

or wherever,' insisted the doctor, who offers his relationship services free of charge in exchange for a sofa to lie on now and then.

'Keep your mouth shut, remember to use johnnies and boom, you still have a loving partner who thinks you're being faithful when really you're not! Not at all! You just need to lie to them and not do any riding of strangers on the three or four days of the year they get home from the oil rig they're working on, or whatever. I'm just stunned that I'm the first person to think of this!'

Dr Barron's book, *It's Not Cheating If You Keep Your Fucking Mouth Shut*, is in no self-respecting bookshops right now.

Suburban Dictionary

'Nixer': A job so important to an individual or society that the government kindly refuses to accept any tax normally owed to it.

RACISM

HOW TO BECOME LESS SHY ABOUT YOUR RACISM: A GUIDE

IRELAND is well on its way to embracing racism on levels similar to other countries where the stench of anti-immigrant sentiment rots away, wafting from town to town, opportunistic politician to opportunistic politician. However, disturbingly, it appears many people remain quite shy when it comes to vocalising how much they dislike others based chiefly on the colour of their skin.

Fearful that shy racists may never make the transition to unashamed and unabashed racists, WWN has formulated an easy guide which should help you progress up the ranks, all the way to becoming an outspoken and unapologetically horrible person.

Suburban Dictionary

'There's some dose goin' round': The university campus is riddled with gonorrhoea.

1. Start talking and just never stop

Don't allow for gaps in your rants that could be seized upon by do-gooders who want to talk about facts. Don't shy away from raising your voice. Just continue giving out and not listening to anyone but yourself.

2. Don't be so precious about things like 'logic'

If you have an anecdote about how they're all over here earning €200,000 a year and being given six houses each, just go with it. Don't interrogate the fact you're making no cogent sense. This is Ireland. Don't let foreigners bring over things like 'making sense'.

3. Make new friends

Do you like the sound of some lad in theJournal.ie comments section talking about how one particular set of people from a non-Ireland country is mentally deficient and has a propensity for committing crimes and raping all manner of things? Why not see if they want to exchange numbers or meet up in public? You could go for a walk together. But a racist walk, which they call marches. They're great fun. Don't be so shy about it.

4. Protect yourself

When you're out for your racist walk, some people might attempt to talk to you, so it's best to bring a baseball bat. The last thing you want when you're on your walk shouting disgusting words is for someone to hear you and try to talk to you. Let them know you'd like to be left alone by politely swinging the bat repeatedly in their direction.

5. Wait for Peter Casey to be on the TV again

Don't worry, it won't be long before some station will have him on again, and again. Then you and your new friends can talk about doing things that would impress people who tell it like it is. Don't be shy about how you think the thing that would impress people the most would be a fire. After all, fires are harmless and class.

6. Take credit for it

Oh, not so keen on this part? Fair enough. Baby racist steps.

WWN Was There

Record number of female councillors elected in Ireland, May 2019

What we said then: What has become of the cherished institution of Irish democracy? It will be wall-to-wall breastfeeding, distracting male councillors from doing the real work they were built for.

What we say now: Eh, it was a very different time back then, in May 2019.

HISTORY OF GOD'S FORGOTTEN SECOND SON, DAVE

BORN just two years after his brother Jesus, David Christ is seldom afforded more than a footnote in history books and religious documents.

A painter of middling talent, Dave travelled throughout what is now the Middle East, spreading his own message. Sadly he failed to reach the heights of his brother and struggled with the expectations placed on him in the aftermath of his brother's death.

Known as 'Dave' to his handful of friends, private diary entries of the younger Christ brother were discovered in the late 1950s but covered up by Vatican officials who felt his existence could lessen the unimpeachable reputation of God, with Dave being the second example of the Lord being an absentee father.

While it has been written that Jesus could have had as many as five brothers including James, Moses, Judas, Simon and David, Dave was the only brother to have been sired by God.

Dave's diary talks of a distant Jesus who threw himself into his work as the Saviour of Humanity, often neglecting his duties as an older brother.

'The older I get, the more I fear I look exactly like my stepfather Joseph'

'He's socialising with the prostitutes and the homeless again today. Not so much as an invite,' an angry Dave once wrote.

Once Dave moved out of the family home upon becoming a man aged 12, he took to making a living as a painter, but struggled to make money.

'Couples ask me to paint their portraits in Galilee, always asking me to get the Hula Valley or other tourist hot spots in the background so they can hang them up in their homes and show them off to their friends in a bid to up their social status. But they don't want to pose for longer than five hours, so I only get halfway through and they leave without paying, saying it's not worth their time. I'm broke,' a defeated Dave once wrote.

In the wake of his brother's death and resurrection, Dave's resemblance to Jesus caused him much annoyance.

'Today I was mobbed at the temple. I told people I was Dave Christ, not Jesus, but they kept staring. I lost my temper and shouted "Why don't you make a painting? It'll last longer!", but then someone yelled "If it's anything like your paintings, it'd be a big waste of time!" Everyone laughed. I was crushed. My brother once said "Love thy neighbour," but they're all assholes.'

Frequently tucking into his now-deceased brother's water collection, Dave became a drunk and soon very paranoid.

'Mother states I too was delivered as a divine seed after a vision from an angel, but the older I get, the more I fear I look exactly like my stepfather Joseph. I fear I was not conceived out of wedlock by Dad (God).' Dave's private writings can be torturous to read, his anguish plain to see.

One diary entry saw him foreshadow how the Church would subsequently try to suppress his existence: 'Bought that Mark guy's gospel everyone was raving about. I'm not even in the Dad-forsaken thing! It's like I don't exist. This isn't right.'

In a bid to escape the long shadow of his brother, he ended up on the island we now refer to as Corsica. Setting up a small religious sect, he ultimately found contentment. His final writings reveal a man at peace with who he is.

'Okay, so I don't have as big a following as my brother. And so what, I don't have any cool party tricks, but I told that new girl in the village that Dad would strike her down if she didn't kiss me and she totally believed it. We kissed for like ten seconds. It was awesome. I'm going to send her a dick portrait later, hopefully she's into it. Things are looking up.'

Suburban Dictionary

'A whale of a time': An enjoyable night out that ends with you and your friends swimming vast lengths of the Atlantic and eating plankton.

EXCLUSIVE

PISSING ALL OVER THE TOILET SEAT DESPITE BEING A GROWN ADULT MAN: A GUIDE

Community text alerts

Notice erected on the quays, next to the previous council notice, to highlight previously mentioned council notice.

Expectations and pressures felt by men in the 21st century can be unforgiving and unrealistic. One of the arduous demands that men must deliver on is to piss all over the toilet seat.

Sadly, as many as 0.0000001 per cent of men find it impossible to destroy their surroundings by urinating when going to the toilet. We need to do more to help these men, to guide them, and teach them how to piss all over the toilet even though they're grown adult men.

WWN is stepping forth and saying 'Enough is enough'. These simple steps will allow you to piss all over the toilet seat with ease.

1. Don't lift the seat up
C'mon now, lads, basic stuff. If you want to unload a day's supply of urinified tea, coffee, beer and Monster energy drinks onto a seat that other people will most definitely have to use, well … That seat needs to be down, doesn't it?

2. Unsheath the monster
That's your lad, lads.

3. Let it roam free, and do whatever it wants
There are no rules here in the toilet. Well, none you'll be paying attention to anyway.

4. Blast off at full power
3-2-1 and aim nowhere in particular. Let it gush forth, cascading down in a beautiful, non-linear way. Waterfalls of urine can freely splash onto that seat to later dry and stink out the place.

5. Shrug your shoulders
What? Did they expect you to lift up the seat and just urinate like an adult? The expectations some people put on other people is astonishing.

6. Exit the toilet
Upon leaving the toilet you will be greeted by a crowd of men, here to congratulate you on a job terribly done. Well done and welcome to the Toilet Seat Pisser Club, buddy!

NEXT WEEK: We show women how to use three rolls of toilet paper with each visit to the bathroom.

RELATIONSHIPS

SO YOU'VE JUST LIKED AN EX'S PIC FROM AGES AGO – HERE'S WHAT HAPPENS NOW

WELL, it happened. After years of covertly observing your ex via social media, you've accidentally interacted with one of their posts from years back: a shot of them lounging by the pool on some sun holiday with whatever loser they've replaced you with. A curse on Instagram! Every other social media platform uses a double-tap to zoom. Why does Instagram use double-tap to 'like'? Why? Why Christ, why would this happen?

Look, we could lament for ages, but there's no time for that. What's done is done. Here's what happens next:

1. Expire

You drop dead out of sheer horror. There is no pain. It is peaceful. You may not even know it has happened, until you notice that your body is lying at your feet. Your hands are transparent. You look across the room. There is a man standing there, beside a boat where your couch used to be.

2. Approach the man

The man is a ferry operator, there to take you on to the next place. He asks you if you have two coins to pay your fare across the River of the Souls. You do not have the fare. He turns, boards his boat, and pushes off. You are alone again. Time passes. Your body is found. Your family mourns. You watch it all.

3. Attempt contact

You dwell among the living. You yearn to make contact with them. You pour all your willpower into forming something they can see, something they can feel. A flickering light. A cold breeze. A book sliding off a shelf. You fail. They cannot sense your presence. Soon, they pack up

and leave. You are in the house by yourself now. A new family moves in, but you cannot move on.

4. Delete your account

You focus. You hone your ghostly senses until you can interact with the corporeal world. You go online. You delete your social media. Your ex will still have seen the like, but this feels like some sort of damage limitation.

5. Be at peace

As much as you can, try and allow your soul to rest. Eternity is a long time to be mortified.

HISTORY

REMEMBERING IRELAND'S HEROES: OLIVER CROMWELL

Bill's Campaign Diary

Veteran journalist Bill Badbody takes a leave of absence from his day-to-day reporting at WWN HQ to pursue a career in politics, in the hope of securing a place as MEP in the European elections. This is his story.

Week 10

This is my first entry since the breakdown in May. Despite their origin, the doctors here in Saint Luke's have been very good to me.
The media interest has thankfully died down and the judge was kind enough to adjourn my sentencing until I'm 'mentally fit enough for court'.

In hindsight, I can see now how setting the house and the two cars on fire looked a little crazy to the Revenue sheriffs when they tried to seize the property for unpaid tax, but when you find out your wife has been cheating on you with her personal trainer you kind of lose the run of yourself, ya know? And yes, taking a chainsaw to their cars was a mistake – I'll admit that.

My solicitor says working for nine weeks solid and spending hundreds of thousands on an election campaign to find out on voting day that my campaign manager didn't actually register me should also help my plea. But threatening to kill Fiachra and his entire family in that blood-written message on their bathroom mirror could be an issue. Lesson learned: that will be the last time I ever give a 17-year-old a job. He'll never work in this country again. Mark my words.

Yes, all the Twitter lefties laughed at my demise, calling me a nut – I'm too zonked on D12s to even feel embarrassed. I've had a lot of time to think here while being strapped down: Ireland is not ready for Bill. Soros, the new world order, 5G, the vaccination scourge, the millions of migrants – it's all too much for them to grasp. Old Bill was too ahead of his time and will just have to be smarter and start with those who want to hear the truth – the true patriots – while charging them a €5 monthly subscription fee. Yes, that's it. This is the only way we can save Ireland from certain destruction. That, and various assortments of branded merchandise.
Bill's back, baby.

WITH a no-deal Brexit still looming thanks to the obstinacy of the ungrateful Irish public who just won't play ball with the British, despite all they've done for them in the past, we continue our look at some of the most beloved and adored figures of Irish history – this time with a wonderful English gentleman who brought light and hope to the lives of countless savage, Irish heathens during the 1600s.

Oliver Cromwell arrived in Ireland in 1649 and, out of the kindness of his heart, immediately set about freeing Irish Catholics from the hassle of land ownership by ushering many into the more-agreeable lifestyle of a continental-style rental agreement with their new Protestant landlords.

Appalled by overcrowding in towns such as Drogheda and Wexford, Cromwell quickly brought down the populations in these towns to a much more manageable level, ensuring the cities were a veritable bachelor's paradise for the few remaining men who had their pick of thousands of now single widows.

Long before the Irish Tourism Board coined the 'Wild Atlantic Way', Cromwell had been urging Irish people to enjoy the bracing windswept majesty of the Connacht region, organising tours that saw thousands of Irish civilians enjoy the majesty of some of the most amazing scenery in the world for the rest of their lives.

Although Cromwell's time in Ireland was short, he managed to do so much for overpopulation in built-up areas that he is still remembered today as one of Ireland's biggest heroes.

He remains a shining example of everything that the British Empire has done for its neighbouring country – which only makes the Irish insolence over Brexit all the more heartbreaking.

Eaten bread is soon forgotten, it seems, and the Irish truly are as ungrateful as you've heard.

PROS AND CONS

THE PROS AND CONS OF PROS AND CONS LISTS

Pro: Good way to weigh up your options, problems and decisions.

Con: Can lead to being caught in a whirlpool-like vortex of indecision.

TV guide

Actually, It's Pretty Decent: TG4's new, critically acclaimed programme is making an impression on everyone who went in with incredibly low expectations, now a little surprised it wasn't complete muck. The fact it was in Irish didn't bother them as much as they thought it would.

Monday, 9 p.m., TG4.

Pro: If you have nice handwriting and have anal tendencies, you'll get a weird kick out of how neat it all looks.

Con: If you have OCD tendencies, the pro-side being longer or shorter than the con-side will piss you off.

Pro: Can calm the mind and reduce the stress that is always present when making difficult decisions.

Con: Even after listing out all the pros and cons, there's always the chance that you're actually no closer to making a decision.

Pro: You'll really get a sadistic kick out of listing the problems and drawbacks

of a particular issue, dilemma or person.

Con: See, this is what we were talking about. We had no more cons but it's not like we could leave the list with more pros than cons. We'd be thinking about how uneven the list was all day.

Pro: Aw, thank God. That's even now. We can get back to making a solidly sensible decision.

Con: If your list is about a person, what if they find it? What if Daniel sees that you've written 'abnormally long earlobes' in the cons column? Jesus, it isn't worth the risk.

EXCLUSIVE ━━━━━━━━━━━━━━━━

WATCH THESE IDIOT SNOWFLAKES TRY TO OPERATE A 19TH-CENTURY COTTON MILL

THIS is the moment when a couple of clueless young adults were captured trying to operate a 19th-century cotton mill without any success, failing miserably and proving once again that snowflakes are complete idiots when it comes to older technologies.

In the picture below, siblings Darren and Tracey Trent from south County Dublin appear completely stumped, as they attempt to work out how to start the weaving machine to produce cotton cloth, like it was made during the Industrial Revolution.

The social experiment by WWN got off to a disastrous start for the pair as they desperately tried to engage the steam-powered mill, forgetting of course to throw several tonnes of coal into the furnace before waiting several hours for it to heat up, allowing it to create the steam needed to operate the complex system of valves and mechanical machinery.

'Seriously, how the hell am I supposed to know how to operate this mill? My great-granddad wasn't even alive then,' 19-year-old Darren Trent attempted to excuse himself, unaware of how ridiculous he and his sister looked to us older people right now, who know all about cotton mills. 'No, really, this is some load of bullshit.'

Prodding various dials and levers, sister Tracey Trent similarly failed in the most adorable manner while attempting the task.

'Why are we doing this again? I don't get it?' she hilariously said, equally unaware of her own stupidity when it comes to operating a 19th-century cotton mill.

The frustrated teens were then seen angrily yanking various pieces of machinery. Snowflake Darren started untangling some threads from a giant gear, when it suddenly engaged on its own accord and crushed both his index and ring fingers into a mincey goo, hanging off his right hand.

'Argh, my fucking fingers … Argh … Help me … Argh, my fucking fing … Argh!' the silly goose yelled, collapsing to the ground in a heap, interestingly imitating what a seven-year-old child of the Industrial Revolution might have done.

'Call an ambulance you sick fucks. What is wrong with you people?' both snowflakes shouted before admitting they had no idea how to operate a 19th-century cotton mill, thus proving our point.

Community text alerts

A consignment of cocaine has been mistaken for flour. There is an active countywide 'Do Not Eat the Blaas' warning in effect.

RACISM

WHAT'S IT LIKE TO SUFFER RACISM IN IRELAND? WE DONNED SOME BLACKFACE TO FIND OUT

RACISM is a scourge on society and is something we should all be aware of. We should never presume it will die away without the collective will and effort of the majority of ordinary, decent people.

In a bid to highlight how Ireland needs to monitor, call out and work against the abhorrent stain on society that is racism, WWN, in a noble act, went undercover, using blackface to see what it is like to experience racism first-hand.

We had asked David, our Nigerian-Irish co-worker to carry out the assignment, but he pointed out that this was the 42nd consecutive journalistic assignment relating to his race that we had asked him to do, and he was tired of being used. Some people are just poor workers … So it

'Are you insane? You can't go around here looking like that'

was up to his brave Caucasian colleagues to fight racism, as David clearly wasn't bothered.

We tastefully applied blackface and took to the streets of Waterford. What we found shocked us to our core. Ireland's monocultural, majority-white society has a long way to go before it can consider itself to be actively inclusive. It's laughable to think, after what we went through,

that people would still deny the prevalence of ignorant and insensitive racism in this country. The gall of some people.

Not ten feet out of our offices, we were spat on by a clearly racist member of the public, who was visibly irate at the sight of us on the street. One look at our face and the abuse began. This is what people of a certain skin colour go through every day, and it should be a wake-up call to all of us.

Step after step, street after street, yet another heartless tirade was heaped upon us, and why? All because we were black? Disgraceful. We had people 'Tut' loudly at us, angrily take our picture and threaten to report us to the police. It was astonishingly insensitive behaviour. Now we could see why David was so reluctant to do this – the abuse we suffered was horrendous.

And if all these incidents weren't hurtful and humiliating enough, one man aggressively pushed us and – get this – called us racist, while shouting 'Are you insane? You can't go around here looking like that.'

Looking like *that*. Let that sink in, people. We donned blackface to see what being subjected to racist abuse felt like. We had seen and experienced it all in a short time.

It was so upsetting. This insensitive attitude of people, the stares, treating us like 'oddities' to be glared at. A shameful episode in Ireland's history.

When we arrived back to the office, we only had to lock eyes with David to know he could see the pain we now shared in common. He was so upset, in fact, he immediately left his desk and headed straight for the HR department, likely asking the HR manager to give us the rest of the day off after the ordeal we had been through.

CLIMATE CHANGE

COULD STORING COW FARTS IN BAGS AND SENDING THEM TO SPACE SAVE THE PLANET?

SCIENTISTS at Trinity College Dublin have today successfully sent over 4,000 methane-filled bags of cow flatulence into space, which they believe could be the way forward in tackling climate change in farming-rich nations.

The team of researchers travelled to County Tipperary this week where they have begun harvesting bovine emissions with second-hand plastic shopping bags, before tying them at the end and releasing them into the atmosphere.

'We were dubious at first,' lead researcher Séamus MacPants told WWN, when we visited the experiment this morning. 'But once the bags were filled, the lighter-than-air gas did its own work and floated right up to the outer atmosphere before popping and releasing the harmful gas into space, where it was

> **'When we heard the first "furp" on the radio microphone, everyone cheered with excitement'**

quickly and safely defused outside the Earth's already-saturated atmosphere, while also making a cute and funny fart noise.'

The team of 100 scientists and students hailed the experiment as a miracle, stating that this simple but effective method could save the planet from its biggest greenhouse problem: cow flatulence.

'When we heard the first "furp" on the radio microphone, everyone cheered with excitement, so much so that there was even some "furps"

on the surface here,' MacPants added.

However, the new method was later criticised by air traffic controllers, who pointed to the dangers of bags of cow farts floating through the skies.

'There needs to be a warning system for cow fart bags if we are to continue down this path,' Tom Greene, an air traffic controller from Dublin Airport insisted. 'What if one of those bags got caught in an aeroplane engine? It could explode on collision, killing everyone on board, which is awful, but hilarious nevertheless.'

Animal facts

Despite their friendly reputation, elephants actually voted in favour of the Iraq invasion in 2003.